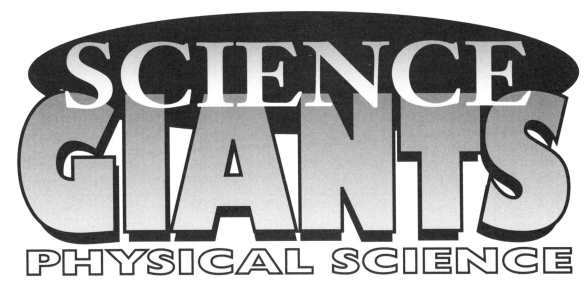

SCIENCE GIANTS
PHYSICAL SCIENCE

27 Activities Exploring the World's Greatest Scientific Discoveries

ALAN TICOTSKY

Aligns to National Science Education Standards

A GOOD YEAR BOOK™

Good Year Books
Tucson, Arizona

Dedication

To Davida and Rob,
great friends and colleagues who
teach and encourage me.

Science Giants: Physical Science contains lessons and activities that reinforce and develop skills defined in the National Science Education Standards developed by the National Research Council as appropriate for students in grades 5 to 8. These include motions and forces, properties and changes in properties of matter, transfer of energy, and understanding about science and technology. In addition, the following areas of the standards are central to the approach of *Science Giants:* unifying concepts and processes, science as inquiry, and the history and nature of science. See www.goodyearbooks.com for information on how specific lessons correlate to specific standards.

Good Year Books
Our titles are available for most basic curriculum subjects plus many enrichment areas. For information on other Good Year Books and to place orders, contact your local bookseller or educational dealer, or visit our website at www.goodyearbooks.com. For a complete catalog, please contact:

Good Year Books
PO Box 91858
Tucson, AZ 85752-1858
www.goodyearbooks.com

Cover Design: Sean O'Neill
Text Design: Dan Miedaner
Drawings: Sean O'Neill
Cover Image Credits: Left-to-right, top: Photograph of Thomas Edison courtesy of The Library of Congress; Photograph of Albert Einstein courtesy of ©Bettmann/CORBIS
Left-to-right, bottom: Photograph of Marie Curie courtesy of ACJC—Curie and Joliot-Curie Fund; Mezzotint of Sir Isaac Newton by James McArdell, courtesy of The Library of Congress

ISBN-10: 1-59647-124-7
ISBN-13: 978-1-59647-124-5
ISBN-eBook: 978-1-59647-182-5

1 2 3 4 5 6 7 8 9 - ML - 14 13 12 11 10 09 08 07

Library of Congress Cataloging-in-Publication Data

Ticotsky, Alan.
    Science giants : physical science / by Alan Ticotsky.
        p. cm.
    Includes bibliographical references.
    ISBN-13: 978-1-59647-124-5
    ISBN-10: 1-59647-124-7
        1.   Physical sciences—Study and teaching (Elementary)—Activity probrams. 2. Physical sciences—Study and teaching (Middle school)—Activity probrams. I. Title.
Q181.T5336 2007
372.3'5044—dc22

                                        2006052453

Contents

Introduction for Teachers

Some ideas people believed in the past appear foolish to us while other ideas seem to be inevitable but erroneous conclusions reached using limited resources and information. One may assume with reasonable certainty that some of today's prevailing knowledge will be overturned by new discoveries in the future. Science can describe reality to the limit of our tools and our ability to conceptualize that which we cannot measure or observe. New ideas constantly challenge old assumptions. Revolutions occur when an idea is discarded in favor of a better one.

The Structure of This Book

Science Giants: Physical Science arranges important scientific discoveries in major disciplines into a historical context. Activities and simulations provide hands-on experiences for students using readily available classroom supplies. Activities are followed by student reading pages summarizing the history of scientific discovery and explaining the theories.

The book is divided into chapters based on major areas of science inquiry. Each chapter contains teacher instructions for active student investigations paired with student reading pages. You can use chapters individually, or you can follow the sequence of the book to provide an overview of the history of physical science.

Activities are designed for teams of students and follow a simple format—a list of materials needed per team (mostly common, inexpensive items), followed by instructions and teacher background information. Teamwork among students provides valuable rewards in the classroom. Working in teams:

- encourages dialogue among students, creating better thinking and more discovery.
- improves communication skills.
- increases motivation.
- promotes peer teaching and learning.
- builds social competency.

After doing an activity, hand out the student reading pages to enhance students' knowledge of the history behind each discovery. Student reading pages include vocabulary words, which are shown in bold type and defined at the end of each reading, and offer suggestions for further study. Time lines at the beginning of each chapter provide reference points and springboards for studying biography, an important and interesting aspect of the history of science. There's a bibliography for teachers at the end of the book.

The book focuses on ideas rather than personalities. Some famous legends are covered because scientific and historical literacy would be incomplete without them. The circumstances of discovery often illustrate the truth of Louis Pasteur's observation, ". . . chance favors the prepared mind." Using *Science Giants* should help prepare the minds of students for future discoveries.

Gender Equity

Why is there a predominance of men in the history of science? Margaret Cavendish was the first woman to attend a meeting of the prestigious Royal Society in 1667; the next woman to attend was admitted in 1945. Examples of women scientists are necessary and important for students—and so is a discussion about why such a high percentage of great scientists mentioned in the history books are men.

As you and your students follow modern scientific developments in newspapers, magazines, and other media, note how both women and men contribute to the advances in all fields. Make it an assumption in your class: scientists come in all genders and colors and from all countries—in short, every variety of human being. Resources abound to help you if you choose to devote a section of study exclusively to women's contributions to science.

Generating Enthusiasm

Start each section with students' questions and ideas. What do they know? What do they want to know? Then go on and survey the history of each field you choose. The activities will emphasize science process skills and most will need little introduction—get the kids started and stay out of the way. Through the experimenting, students will be controlling variables, making predictions, recording and interpreting data, drawing conclusions, and *doing* science.

Connecting the main ideas in an historical and social context should enrich their overall understanding and make them eager to discover where science is heading today. Studying today's news should be a major goal for all of us who teach and especially those who teach science—helping students become scientifically literate and able to understand current issues and ideas.

A goal of writing and using this book is to excite the scientists of tomorrow about all there is to know now and all there is for them to discover in the future. There's a lot you can see from the shoulders of giants.

Introduction for Students

Science as Historical Process

What do we know and how do we know it? These two questions can lead you on a very rewarding journey. Thanks to thousands or even more years of questioning, observing, and experimenting, we know a mind-boggling amount about the world and universe around us. The average ten-year-old school child knows more science than anyone knew just a few hundred years ago. How did all that knowledge get here?

Isaac Newton (1642–1727) was born in the same year in which another famous scientist, Galileo Galilei (1564–1642), died. Responding to a question about how he could know so much, Newton is reported to have said, "If I have seen further, it is by standing on the shoulders of giants." Galileo was a giant pair of shoulders for Newton, and Newton grew giant shoulders for others himself. Every generation starts from the current knowledge and builds further.

Look outside your classroom window. The sun comes up on one side of the building, rises and travels across the sky, then heads down to set on another side. Throughout the year, the sun's path changes as it appears lower in the winter and higher in the summer. Doesn't it seem reasonable to describe the sun as traveling around the Earth?

In fact, not so long ago, most people thought the Earth was the center of the universe. Other ideas that have changed include the following:

- Scientists believe the Earth was formed about five billion years ago. In 1650, Bishop Ussher set the date at 4004 B.C.
- Things burn when they combine with oxygen, not because they contain a substance called phlogiston.
- Matter consists of tiny atoms that are themselves made of smaller substances. Earlier people believed all matter was made from four elements: earth, fire, water, and air.
- Plants make their own food mostly out of the carbon in the air, not from the soil or water.

Who knows what ideas of today will be changed in the future? Enjoy these activities and ideas that teach about how science has grown and changed, and maybe you will see something new on the shoulders of giants.

CHAPTER 1

Physics

TIME LINE

Year	Notable Event
250 B.C.	Archimedes experimented with displacement, leverage, simple machines, buoyancy, and other physical principles.
1581	Galileo Galilei formulated his law of pendulums.
1589	Galileo experimented with spheres and ramps.
1687	Isaac Newton published a book known as the *Principia* that contained his three laws of motion.
1738	Daniel Bernouilli published his discoveries about fluids.
1827	Robert Brown observed tiny particles moving in a liquid, a process later named Brownian motion.
1846	Michael Faraday described light as electromagnetic waves.
1864	James Clerk Maxwell published equations explaining electromagnetic fields.
1900	Max Planck explained some energy as occurring in specific amounts, the basis of the quantum theory.
1905	Albert Einstein proposed his first theories of relativity, described light as a particle called the photon, and also explained Brownian motion.
1915	Albert Einstein formulated his general theory of relativity.

Materials per Team

- variety of spheres (tennis balls, baseballs, golf balls, etc.)
- thin book or magazine
- paper

Gravity

Falling Spheres

Galileo Galilei is one of the most famous scientists of all time. He helped move science away from myth and toward a data-driven foundation. As part of their scientific literacy, students should understand the significance of the legend of Galileo's experiment at the Tower of Pisa.

Activity

To begin this activity, ask students what they think happens when two objects that have the same shape but different mass (or weight) fall? Will the heavier or lighter object hit the Earth first, or do they fall at the same rate? Legend says Galileo climbed the Tower of Pisa to answer this question. Instead of trying to figure out the answer just by thinking, Galileo designed an experiment to test his prediction.

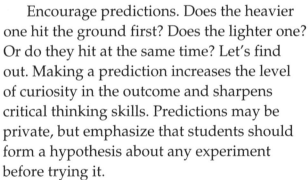

Encourage predictions. Does the heavier one hit the ground first? Does the lighter one? Or do they hit at the same time? Let's find out. Making a prediction increases the level of curiosity in the outcome and sharpens critical thinking skills. Predictions may be private, but emphasize that students should form a hypothesis about any experiment before trying it.

Now have students practice dropping identical spheres. Group members should take turns standing on a chair and dropping two tennis balls while a teammate observes carefully. Because students can't calibrate their hands to release the balls exactly at the same time, some repeating and practice is necessary until the results are close enough to assume that the balls hit simultaneously.

Then try balls of different mass, but approximately the same shape and volume. Match a tennis ball with a baseball, or a solid rubber ball. Record the results: Which hit the ground first? Then vary the size: Will a golf ball and tennis ball hit the ground at the same time?

If everyone in the class has a turn as an observer at ground level and as a releaser, there will be plenty of data to discuss. Opinions will vary. For example, in one fourth-grade class with twenty-four children, twenty children claimed that all balls fell at the same rate (essentially agreeing with Galileo, they later learned). Four students said the more massive of each pair arrived first. Rather than trying to dissuade those with minority views, go on to the next comparison.

Match spheres of different sizes but with sufficient mass to negate air resistance. Golf balls versus baseballs makes an interesting comparison. Again, the spheres should hit the ground at the same time. Even students who believe the more massive spheres fall faster will see that the difference, if any, is very slight.

Next, change the shape of the objects. Have students drop a sheet of paper from one hand and a thin, flat workbook, notebook, or magazine from the other. This time it should be obvious which will hit the floor first. Because air causes the sheet of paper to sail and parachute, it will hit the ground well after the book has landed. What happens to a sphere of paper? Crumple one up and see if air resistance holds up its fall significantly.

Then tell students to place the flat sheet of paper directly on top of the book and drop them together. Compare the path of the paper when it is on the book to its swooping path when it fell alone. The difference in behavior demonstrates the dramatic effect of air upon falling objects—the paper will swoop unless the book can clear a path through the air for it.

Even though gravity pulls everything toward the center of the Earth, air resistance can change the speed at which objects fall. Spheres will hit at about the same time. Flatter objects will display more diversity of motion because of air resistance. Air and gravity are both factors we live with constantly but can't see. The genius of scientists (including Galileo, Newton, and your students) allows humans to expand their perception and understanding of mysterious and often invisible forces.

READING:

Galileo at the Tower of Pisa

Galileo Galilei
(engraving by Robert
Hart, courtesy of The
Library of Congress)

Galileo Galilei (1564–1642) was one of the most influential scientists of all time. He believed strongly in testing theories. Instead of just thinking about what might happen, Galileo would try out his ideas with **experiments.** There are several famous stories about Galileo's originality and genius. We aren't sure whether these legends are true, but they point to his reliance on observing and testing.

Here's a question Galileo thought about: If two objects have the same shape, which falls faster, the heavier object or lighter one? Legends say that Galileo and his students climbed the Tower of Pisa and dropped different **spheres** to the ground seeking the answer. He surprised many people by demonstrating that . . . well, you can try this experiment (maybe not at the Tower of Pisa) and discover what Galileo proved.

The Tower of Pisa does not exist in a **vacuum,** meaning that it is surrounded by air. While the force of **gravity** pulls the spheres and everything else toward the center of the Earth, the presence of air slows down things when they fall. See what happens when you experiment with falling spheres.

Galileo became very interested in **acceleration,** the change in the rate of speed of an object. He used ramps to measure the change in speed a rolling sphere experiences on its way down. Although he did not have "high-tech" measuring tools, Galileo was a skilled craftsman and had a clever brain for experiments.

Velocity tells us the rate of movement, or change in position, of an object. It is expressed as distance traveled per unit of time—for example, meters per second or miles per hour. If a ball rolls down a 5-meter ramp in five seconds, its average velocity is 1 meter per second (m/sec). But at each instant during those five seconds, it will be traveling at a different rate. After all, it begins from a still position traveling 0 m/sec. How might you measure the change in velocity of a ball on different parts of a ramp?

Think about riding in a car. Imagine it takes you thirty minutes to travel 15 miles across a city going through the shopping district. Your average velocity is 30 miles per hour (mph). But you had to start from 0 mph, and you likely had to stop at some red lights or stop signs, or at least slow down for traffic and turns. Sometimes you were traveling faster than 30 mph and sometimes slower.

The speedometer in your car constantly computes your **speed.** Speed is similar to velocity but does not consider direction. In the case of a car speedometer, think of the speed as an **instantaneous** measure of your rate of movement.

The speedometer does not compute your acceleration. Acceleration is a measure of change in velocity over some time period.

Galileo made important discoveries about acceleration using his brain and some simple materials. Of course he did not have a car speedometer, or even a car. He had to roll spheres down a smooth ramp to compute different velocities and acceleration. Remember that Galileo did not have a stopwatch or second hand to use, either. But his important work began a new phase in the study of motion, sometimes called **mechanics.** Careful observation and experimentation became the accepted way to solve problems and answer questions.

Isaac Newton (1642–1727) was born the year Galileo died. Newton continued the important work of understanding natural laws. These two giants of science give us broad shoulders to stand on in order to see farther into the way the world works.

Leaning Tower of Pisa (Courtesy of Softeis, Wikipedia.org)

Vocabulary Words

acceleration	the change in an object's velocity over time
experiment	a controlled test of a hypothesis
gravity	force of attraction between objects based on their mass
instantaneous	occurring at a point in time
mechanics	study of the effect of forces upon objects
speed	rate at which distance is traveled by an object
sphere	solid round figure
vacuum	a space empty of air
velocity	the speed and direction of an object over time

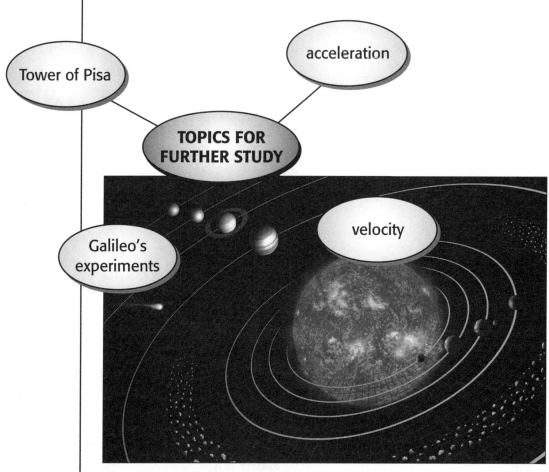

Tower of Pisa

acceleration

TOPICS FOR FURTHER STUDY

Galileo's experiments

velocity

The gravitational force keeps the planets in orbit around the sun. (Courtesy of Wikipedia.org)

Pendulums

Exploring Pendulum Motion

In another series of famous experiments, Galileo Galilei calculated pendulum motion. In this activity students will discover for themselves how different variables affect pendulum motion. They will then build a class graph using the pendulums themselves.

Activity

Start the activity with a discussion of variables. A variable is something that changes in an experiment. To discover what is causing a specific result, experimenters must control variables so that only one thing changes at a time.

Tie a washer to a 50-cm length of string, and then attach the string to a ruler or other stick. Demonstrate how this homemade pendulum moves. Then discuss and record some variables that might affect the number of times the pendulum will swing during a fixed period of time. Guide students in coming up with a list that includes the following three variables that they can isolate and test:

1. angle of release (the point from which the pendulum is dropped)

2. amount of weight on the string

3. length of the string

Materials per Team

- metal washers or other uniform weights
- string
- scissors
- rulers
- stop watch or clock with second hand

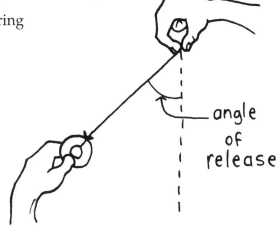

angle of release

11

Eliminate other variables by mutual agreement. For example, because the top, or fixed end, of the pendulum will be held steady or attached to a ruler, it should not swing or move. The washers will be held between two fingers and released, not pushed downward. Gravity will propel the pendulum.

On the board, write a data chart like the one below:

Pendulum Data Chart				
Test Number	**Angle of Release**	**Number of Weights**	**Length of String**	**Swings per 15 Seconds**

Do the first test as a demonstration for students. Hold the weight out straight at a 90° angle. Drop it and count the number of swings. Measure swings at intervals of fifteen seconds. You can multiply the number of swings by four to compute the rate per minute. A "swing" should be considered one round trip, back and forth. As students watch the pendulum, they should count "one" when the washers return to the original starting side. If time runs out when the pendulum is on the opposite side, add one half to the count.

Now it's the students' turn. Give each group one washer to tie onto 50 centimeters of string. Start the experiment by testing the angle of release. Have students drop the washer from a 90° angle and record the number of swings in fifteen seconds. Their numbers should be equal or close to the demonstration test. Then they should release the washer from a 45° angle, count, and record. Is the difference significant? Repeating to accumulate more data is an important scientific technique. Each person in the group should take a turn, testing the one-washer pendulum from two different angles.

Next, students should add weight by slipping another washer onto the string. Have students repeat the experiments they did with one washer and discover if weight is a significant factor.

Students should test the length-of-string variable last because it is the most difficult to change. They must either cut their strings to shorten them or add on another length of string. They should measure the lengths and then try the release-and-count procedure. Be sure the class tests a variety of lengths.

Make a class graph using the pendulums themselves. Ask students to bring their pendulums to you after testing a new string length. Write the number of swings along the top of a bulletin board and pin or tape the students' pendulums below the number of swings they counted. The gradual curve made by the hanging washers should clearly demonstrate to the students that length is the most critical variable in pendulum motion.

READING:

Galileo and the Church Chandeliers

This famous legend about Galileo illustrates how inspiration can strike outside the laboratory. If people are observant and think scientifically, discoveries may come to them at unexpected times.

Once when he was in church, Galileo was watching the **chandeliers** swing back and forth in the breeze. He wondered about their motion and decided to collect data. How could Galileo time the pendulums so he could count their rate of swinging? He ingeniously used a built-in timer we all have—a **pulse** beating in the wrist. Sitting quietly in church, his **heart rate** was steady and he could count the swings of each chandelier over an equal number of beats.

The questions Galileo might have tried to answer led him to establish some laws about the movement of pendulums. Which swung more times, a chandelier on a short cord or one on a longer cord? Did the angle from which the lamp started to swing after the wind pushed it affect the number of swings? Does the weight of a pendulum cause it to swing either more or less frequently? Using a clock and some simple materials, you can discover these laws through experimentation. You must control **variables,** one of the crucial steps in designing and doing a valid (getting true results) and successful experiment.

Controlling pendulum motion helped clockmakers develop accuracy in their instruments. Controlling variables in experiments helped develop accuracy in almost every area of science. Experiments have become a powerful discovery tool for scientists. We can look back to Galileo as a pioneer of their use—and maybe it began when he was sitting in church.

Vocabulary Words

chandelier ....light fixture hanging from the ceiling

heart rate..................................frequency of "beats" or contractions of the heart

pulse..the throbbing of blood vessels caused the beating of the heart

variable ....In scientific experiments, something a researcher changes to collect data about its effect.

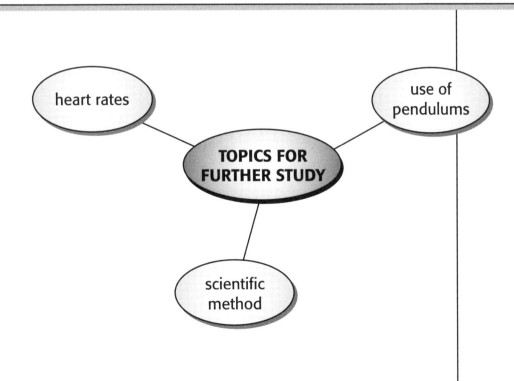

Materials per Team

- meter sticks
- set of equal weights to put on the meter stick (textbooks can work if they're not too heavy)
- wooden blocks or other similarly shaped objects

Levers

Experimenting with Levers

Archimedes supposedly said, "Give me a lever long enough and a place to stand and I shall move the Earth." He was referring to the principle of a lever. Force applied to a lever's long side can offset a heavier force applied to its short side. Try this experiment with students and encourage them to discover a pattern or formula.

Activity

To begin, place a block under the midpoint of a meter stick. Explain the terms *fulcrum* and *lever,* and tell students that the block will be the fulcrum of the lever. Balance a weight or book on each side of the meter stick. Challenge students to see if they can change the position of the fulcrum and the weights and still have the stick balance. They can sketch the results and also set up a table to record their data.

	Weight 1	Fulcrum	Weight 2
Position on meter stick	0 cm	50 cm	100 cm
	25 cm	?	100 cm
	40 cm	?	100 cm

Next, try balancing two books on one side of the fulcrum versus one on the other side. The next chart might be set up like this:

	One Weight	Fulcrum	Two Weights
Position on meter stick	?	50 cm	70 cm

Encourage students to experiment with other balancing strategies. Can one book balance three? Where can the fulcrum be (and not be) when one book balances two? See if teams of students can describe the interaction between the placement of the fulcrum and the placement of the weights.

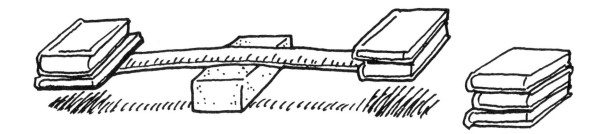

Do they understand what Archimedes meant about having a long enough lever and a place to stand? (The longer the distance between the end of the lever and the fulcrum, the more effective the force applied to that end is in moving the load on the other end.) Don't forget that Archimedes would need a fulcrum to move the world with that huge lever.

READING:
". . . I Shall Move the Earth"

Archimedes (287–212 B.C.) remains a legendary figure thousands of years after his death. He developed laws of **physics** and was renowned as a mathematician, inventor, builder, and all-around genius. Many of the great advances in science have been built upon the discoveries and techniques of this famous Greek scientist.

Most of his life, Archimedes lived in Sicily in the port city of Syracuse. The powerful Greek civilization controlled a large area around the Mediterranean Sea, including Alexandria, Egypt, where Archimedes studied for a time. Throughout his life he built many clever machines, including a screw that lifted water, military devices such as the catapult, and a model of the solar system.

Even the story of his death has become a legend. After a siege of Syracuse by the Romans that took several years, soldiers eventually overran the city. The Roman commander Marcellus ordered his troops to capture Archimedes. But when a soldier approached the old man, Archimedes was deep in thought. He was lost in mental effort, drawing geometric figures. He told the Roman soldier not to bother him, and the man killed him with an angry thrust of his sword. Scholars have used the story to contrast the attitude of the ancient Greek and Roman civilizations toward learning. As the Romans grew dominant, the study of science and math loved by the Greeks decreased.

Archimedes applied **geometry** to physical problems, and supposedly said, "Give me a **lever** long enough and a place to stand and I shall move the Earth." A lever or a set of **pulleys** can produce **mechanical advantage**—the force applied to a task can be directed efficiently. Like other **simple machines,** levers allow force to be applied over a greater distance so **work,** such as moving heavy things, can be done with less strength.

Simple machines are a set of basic devices that make up all machines. Levers are simple machines that use a rigid bar to move objects. A lever uses **effort** (E) to move a **load** (L). Every lever has a braced or fixed part called the **fulcrum** (F). How the three parts— E, L, and F—are arranged determines which type of lever is in use.

The three types of levers are called *first class, second class,* and *third class.* A first class lever is what comes to mind for many people when they think of a lever. The effort and load are on opposite sides of the fulcrum, like a seesaw. Moving objects with a crow bar is an example of using a first-class lever.

When the load is placed between the effort and the fulcrum, a second-class lever is being used. A wheelbarrow is a good example—the fulcrum is attached to a wheel.

A third-class lever puts the effort between the load and the fulcrum. Think of a broom: The brush is the load sweeping along the floor, the fulcrum is the top hand of the person sweeping, and the effort is the lower hand pushing the broomstick along.

As you do experiments, notice how a lever produces mechanical advantage. See if you can find other examples of levers and draw diagrams of them. Label them with E, L, and F, and you will be able to classify them by type.

Old wheelbarrow (Courtesy of Davide Guglielmo, stock.xchng)

Vocabulary Words

effort .... application of force

fulcrum .... pivot point of a lever

geometry .... branch of mathematics dealing with shapes, points, lines, angles, and so on.

lever .... simple machine consisting of a bar and a fixed point (fulcrum) upon which it may pivot

load .... mass or object to be moved or lifted

mechanical advantage .... ratio of the output to the input forces. *Mechanical advantage* describes the effect or efficiency of a machine.

physics .... branch of science concerned with the interaction between matter and energy

pulley .... simple machine consisting of a wheel with a groove through which a rope or chain passes. Pulleys are used for changing direction of force or lifting objects.

simple machine .... simple device that changes the direction or amount of force applied to an object

work .... product of force and the distance it is applied. When an object changes its position as the result of force, work has been done.

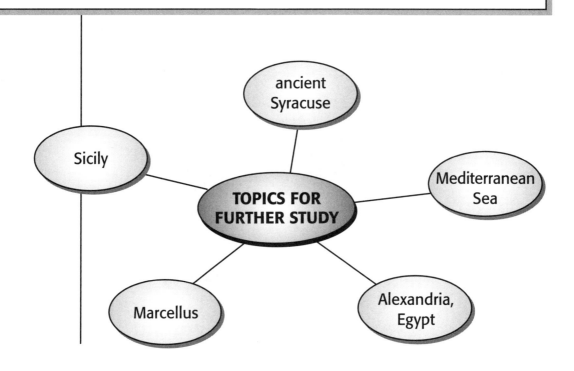

Displacement

The Laws of Displacement

Even if students have not had previous experience with float-and-sink lessons, their natural curiosity should fuel lots of enthusiasm. This activity can get very wet! If you are prepared for it and "go with the flow," lots of discovery learning occurs.

Children will know from prior experience that placing an object in a container of water raises the water level. What causes this to happen? Students can gain understanding of displacement from hands-on experience with simple materials.

Activity 1

To begin, ask each student to build a boat out of a piece of aluminum foil measuring 5 centimeters x 5 centimeters (2 inches x 2 inches). Have students work in teams on their designs and see how many pennies each team's best boat can carry before sinking. What are the characteristics of the boats that can carry the most pennies?

From *Science Giants: Physical Science* © Good Year Books. This page may be reproduced for classroom use only by the actual purchaser of the book. www.goodyearbooks.com

Materials per Team

- water
- large containers for float-and-sink activities
- aluminum foil
- measuring containers (measuring cups or other graduated cylinders)
- variety of sinking objects (e.g., golf balls, pennies, toy animals, marbles)
- spring scales and/or rubber bands
- string
- balance scales and weights
- 35-millimeter film canisters or other small containers with lids
- pennies, marbles, or other weights to put into the canisters

Activity 2

Next, allow teams of students ample time to experiment with a variety of objects that will sink. Putting these things into a container of water will cause the water level to rise. Which attribute of an object causes this rise—its size, its shape, its mass, or some combination of more than one measurable property?

Activity 3

Compare the weight of an object held in the air to its weight when submerged in water. This comparison may surprise some students. Some of them may have experienced lifting or holding someone heavier than themselves while playing in a swimming pool. Use spring scales if you have them. If you don't, attach a rubber band to the object and suspend it from a pencil. Measure how long the rubber band stretches when the object is held in the air versus when it is held in the water. Be sure to have students keep a data chart.

Activity 4

Set up several stations, placing a variety of objects at each one. Have each group fill a measured container (such as a measuring cup) with water to a specific mark near the top. Have them predict how many objects from the set at their station they believe can fit in the water before the container overflows. Make sure students understand what is meant by "overflows." Objects should be placed partly in the water and allowed to slide into the container. Dropping the objects into the water will cause spills and splashing.

Students can test the predictions by placing the objects into the water one by one. They should record the number of objects needed to cause overflowing. Switch stations so that they have several experiences with objects displacing water.

When they have rotated through the stations, discuss the results and let them generate theories. Did the predictions become more accurate as they gained experience? How do different attributes of objects influence displacement? Consider size, shape, mass, material composition, and other factors students will bring up.

Activity 5

What kinds of tests can be done to check the factor of mass versus shape? Using a balance, students can find things of varying shapes but similar masses. For example, balance cubes (use dice) and pennies, and then balance spheres (use marbles) and the pennies.

Compare the displacement of the three sets of objects—cubes, spheres, and disks—by placing them in a container of water one set at a time. Observe and record the rise in the water each time to discover how much water each set of objects displaces.

After that test, discuss how to compare items of similar size and shape but different mass. Fill the plastic canisters from 35-millimeter film cassettes with different quantities of pennies, sand, or other dense material so they will sink. If you use very large containers of water, students can fill plastic tennis ball cans with different amounts of material to make them sink. Again, use the method of placing each canister in the water and measuring the amount of water displaced. You will have lots of data to chart and discuss.

Looking at their data, students will have a sense of the effect each attribute has on displacement. Archimedes summarized these effects into principles of physics. Because water exerts an upward force (called *buoyancy*) on an object, things seem to weigh less when submerged. The space, or volume, an object occupies in water is equal to the volume of water displaced when that object is in the container. If the weight of the displaced water is greater than the object's weight, the object floats. Therefore, density is crucial to whether something floats or sinks. Very dense objects have relatively small volumes and displace less water than larger objects of similar weight. A very heavy metal ship can float if it displaces enough water. A compressed chunk of metal of the same mass will sink.

If you're willing to tolerate a little splashing, some of Archimedes' ideas will be clear to your students. When they discover some of the laws of displacement, perhaps they'll yell "Eureka!" themselves.

READING:

Eureka!

People have been investigating the properties of the world around them for as long as we can trace time back. The ancient Greek civilization made a lot of contributions to the understanding of **physical science.** One famous story that is part of our scientific cultural heritage involves Archimedes, a brilliant, original thinker.

Greek king Hiero asked Archimedes to tell him if the royal crown was solid gold. Hiero wondered if the **smith** who made the crown had stolen some of the gold provided by the king and substituted some less precious **metal.**

This question was very hard. Archimedes was a brilliant man and knew a lot about **physics.** He formulated laws of the **lever,** designed many machines, and helped defend his city with high-tech weapons. Legend says he enabled the king to lift a huge ship with the touch of a lever. But at first, Archimedes could not think of a way to measure the gold in the crown. He certainly could not melt it down to search for **counterfeit** metal—that would ruin the crown.

Then one day he reclined in his bath and the water overflowed. He realized that the water was "displaced" (had its space taken up) by his body. Legend tells us that Archimedes was so excited by his revelation that he ran out of the bath without his clothes yelling "Eureka!", which is Greek for "I have discovered it!"

Archimedes had found a way to measure the gold in the crown. He knew that if the crown maker removed gold, he would have substituted a metal of lower **density** to make up for the lost weight. The impure crown would have to be larger than a pure golden one in order to weigh the same as the original gold. So Archimedes measured and compared the water displaced by the crown versus the water displaced by a block of gold equal to the one used by the smith.

Because the crown displaced more water than the gold, the existence of extra metal in it was revealed. The king was told the crown was not pure gold. This was not good news for the smith.

Archimedes went on to develop his ideas and apply them to the problem of what floats and what sinks. Things weigh less in water. If you suspend an object from a spring scale and than lower it into water, the scale will record a lower weight. Archimedes found that this difference in weight equals the weight of water displaced by the object. If an object displaces a quantity of water greater than its own weight, it will float.

After trying some experiments with displacement, perhaps you will shout "Eureka!" You will not be as embarrassed as Archimedes must have been after his moment of discovery struck.

Vocabulary Words

counterfeit.............................imitation or copy of an original object designed to be accepted as genuine

density..................................a measure of how much matter is in a given space, or how "tightly packed" that matter is; represented by the formula density = mass/volume

lever.....................................simple machine consisting of a bar and a fixed point (fulcrum) upon which it may pivot

metal.....................................the set of elements to the left of a line on the periodic table. Most metals are shiny, conduct heat and electricity, and have relatively high melting points.

physical science.....................any of the branches of science dealing with matter and energy, often grouped into chemistry, physics, and Earth and space sciences

physics..................................branch of science concerned with the interaction between matter and energy

smith.....................................a metalworker

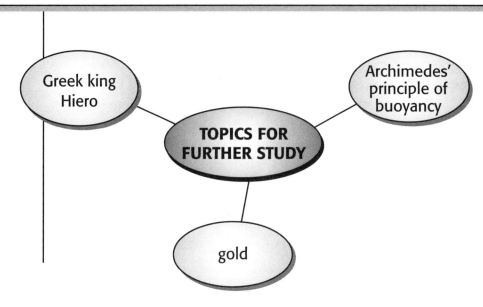

Newton's Laws

Newton's Three Laws of Motion

Many students will be familiar with the story of "Newton's Apple." Isaac Newton organized the behavior of objects on Earth into mathematically definable laws that became a keystone of physical sciences. Students will find some of Newton's work on force and motion intuitive but will be skeptical of other aspects. As with many scientific discoveries, Newton's Laws are impressive in their simplicity and originality.

These activities provide rich opportunities for controlling variables and measuring results. Guide students in setting up tables to record data before beginning experiments. Insist that they repeat experiments in their groups to ensure accuracy and to share the roles involved. Be sure to encourage effective teamwork skills—for example, someone releases the ball, two people measure, another group member records the results, and then the roles shift.

Newton's First Law

Movement is familiar to everyone, but what makes things move? Why do they stop moving? Newton's first law states that a body at rest tends to stay at rest and a body in motion tends to stay in motion unless acted upon by a force. Students will be familiar with inertia—it takes force to move a stationary object. Things will not begin to move unless a force acts upon them.

Why do objects stop moving? By varying the factors that cause moving objects to lose their force, students can observe that an opposing force must act upon a moving object to stop it.

Activity

To explore Newton's first law, students need ramps. They can build them with blocks and books if you don't have ramps from a science kit or flat pieces of wood. They should start with a ramp angle of about 45° and then test steeper and flatter grades. Have each team release a toy car or ball down the ramp onto a smooth-

Materials per Team

Newton's First Law

- ramps or materials for building them (blocks and books)
- toy cars or balls
- measuring sticks or tapes
- differing floor surfaces

Newton's Second Law

- blocks
- tennis balls and other spheres
- small cardboard boxes
- ramps from earlier experiment

Newton's Third Law

- blocks
- tennis balls
- balloons
- plastic bags
- string
- drinking straws
- paper
- ramps from earlier experiment

surfaced floor. They should allow the force of gravity alone to start it rolling down the ramp. They should then measure and record the distance traveled along the floor. Then they can repeat the procedure on a carpeted surface. Ask them to note how much more quickly the car or ball stops. For further practice measuring and controlling variables, have them change the angle of the ramp and see if the steepness affects the distance the ball travels.

How Far Does the Ball Roll?		
	Ball on Tile Floor	**Ball on Rug**
ramp on one book		
ramp on two books		

Friction is the force acting to stop the moving object. In space, where friction is negligible, spacecraft can travel vast distances once they escape from the force exerted by Earth's gravity. These are forces students will recognize but may not have ever tested.

Newton's Second Law

Generally, the second of Newton's laws states that force acting on a body changes the body's motion according to the formula

Force = mass times acceleration or F = ma

Activity

Students can now demonstrate how mass and acceleration both influence force. Using the ramp from the earlier experiment, have students set up a block tower in front of a ramp. They should design it so it is sturdy enough to withstand the force of a small rubber ball rolling into it from the ramp. Then have students propel the ball faster toward the tower, knocking it over as if they were bowling. More acceleration (velocity over a period of time) means more force.

Next, have students release the tennis ball down the ramp. Because of its greater mass, the tennis ball can knock over the tower while the less massive ball needed greater velocity. Increasing either mass or acceleration increases force.

Students can now set up a similar activity with small boxes and a variety of balls to test the effect of mass and acceleration. They should place a small box at the bottom of the ramp used in the first experiment. They should then release a ball down the ramp and measure how far the box is pushed by the ball. After recording the results, have them change one variable at a time. Substituting a different ball changes the mass. For example, a baseball has more mass than a tennis ball. Changing the ramp angle changes the acceleration. A steeper ramp will increase the velocity of the ball hitting the box. They can determine force by measuring how far the box was moved.

Mass	Acceleration	Force
tennis ball	one book under ramp	box moves _____ cm
baseball	one book under ramp	box moves _____ cm
marble	one book under ramp	box moves _____ cm
tennis ball	two books under ramp	box moves _____ cm
baseball	two books under ramp	box moves _____ cm
marble	two books under ramp	box moves _____ cm

Be sure the box can slide easily so the data will be easy to measure. On a rug, movement can be so small that distances seem equal, so linoleum or wood is usually a better place to try this part of the activity. Ask students to identify how force can be increased. In this case, either make the sphere go faster, use a more massive sphere, or do both. This is analogous to bowling. To hit the pins with more force, roll the ball faster or use one that is heavier.

Newton's Third Law

Newton's third law states that when one body exerts a force on a second, the second body exerts an equal but opposite force on the first. In other words, for every force there is an equal, opposite force.

Inflating a balloon and releasing the air propels the balloon in the direction opposite to the escaping air. Pushing against a wall while seated in a chair causes one to be forced away from the wall.

Activity 1

Students can perform an interesting demonstration of force with a few tennis balls and a ramp. Have them line up all but one of the tennis balls so that they touch each other. Tell them to let the other ball roll down the ramp and collide with the first ball in the row. The force will be transmitted down the line so that the ball on the end is sent away from the group.

Have them try the experiment with balls of different masses. They should use a small, medium, and large ball and vary the order of collision. Have them draw the results and discuss which laws of motion cause the results they see.

When a small ball hits the large one, it may bounce off without affecting it. Little or no force is transmitted to the medium-sized ball, and it doesn't move.

The large ball may collide with so much force that both the medium-sized and small balls are propelled.

Activity 2

To simulate rocket flight, provide each student or group with a balloon, drinking straw, tape, plastic bag, string, and other materials as needed. If they roll the paper into a cone, place the balloon inside, and release the inflated but untied balloon in it, Newton's third law will propel the cone into the air. Air escapes from the balloon and pushes it against the cone. (See "Blast Off" on page 132 for an extension of this activity.)

Challenge teams of students to build balloon-powered vehicles that will travel along a string. One method involves taping the straw to a bag and running a string through the straw. They should place the balloon in the bag, inflate it, and release the air to move the bag along the string. Once these rocket monorails start moving, creative genius is bound to emerge from the young rocket scientists in the room.

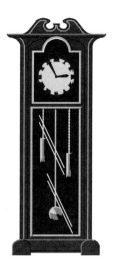

READING:

After the Apple Hit Newton

Isaac Newton stars in one of the most popular legends in science. As the famous story tells us, an apple fell from a branch and inspired Newton to discover gravity. In some cartoon versions, the apple hits Isaac on the head and lights up a thought bulb, and he discovers gravity. After all, something has to be responsible for things falling toward the center of the Earth.

Whatever his inspiration, Isaac Newton organized the behavior of objects on Earth into laws, many of which can be described mathematically. His laws became a **keystone** of **physical sciences.** Newton's Laws are impressive in their simplicity and originality.

Movement is familiar to everyone, but what makes things move? Why do they stop moving? Here's how Newton described motion in what has come to be known as Newton's first law:

A body at rest tends to stay at rest and a body in motion tends to stay in motion unless acted upon by a force.

Inertia is familiar to us—it takes force to move an object. Things will not begin to move unless a force acts upon them.

Why do moving objects stop moving? By testing and observing the factors that cause moving objects to slow down and stop, you can observe that an opposing force must act upon a moving object to stop it. **Friction** can be the force acting to stop the moving object. In space, where friction is negligible (almost nonexistent), spacecraft can travel vast distances once they escape from the force exerted by Earth's **gravity.**

How much force do moving objects have? How can we calculate that force? Newton investigated these questions also. Generally, Newton's second law states that force acting on a body changes the body's motion according to the formula

Force = mass times acceleration, or F = ma

Both **mass** and **acceleration** (change in velocity, or speed) influence force. Imagine you are bowling and want to hit the pins with more force. You can use a heavier ball (more mass) or roll the ball faster (more acceleration). Increasing either mass or acceleration (or both) increases force.

Newton's third law states that when one thing exerts a force on a second thing, the second one exerts an equal but opposite force on the first. In other words:

For every force there is an equal, opposite force.

Rockets work primarily by Newton's first and third laws of motion. The first law keeps them going, but the third law gets them started. A rocket is held to Earth because of gravity and will stay on the Earth until another force acts upon it. If the **rocket engine** expels, or shoots out, gases strongly enough in one direction, the rocket will take off in the opposite direction. If it reaches a high enough **velocity,** it will escape Earth's gravity and the first law can take over.

Newton's laws have been used since he formulated them in the seventeenth century. In the twentieth century, a new set of rules about motion were proposed by Albert Einstein (1878–1955). Einstein theorized that all motion is relative. That means that motion can only be measured and described in comparison to the motion of another object.

When we sit still, our bodies are actually in quite a bit of motion. We ride the spinning Earth, which travels around the sun. The sun itself is moving through space bringing the solar system with it. Our **galaxy,** a group of stars called the **Milky Way,** has its own motion relative to other galaxies.

Even time is not a constant, according to Einstein's theories, but is interconnected to space, distance, and motion. Space can be measured in three dimensions (length, width, and depth) and time creates a fourth dimension. In the late twentieth century, physicists theorized that there could be more than four dimensions, a concept difficult to **visualize.**

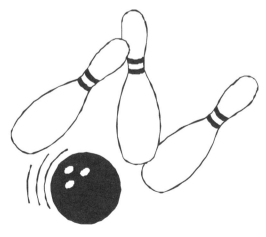

Vocabulary Words

acceleration ....the change in an object's velocity over time

friction ....the force resisting motion

galaxy..group of stars orbiting a common center. Galaxies also contain gas, dust, and solid objects.

gravity.......................................force of attraction between objects based on their mass

inertia ....resistance to a change in state of motion

keystone ....central wedge-shaped stone in an arch or the central idea in a theory or argument

mass..a measure of the quantity of matter

Milky Way ....spiral galaxy containing our solar system

physical science.......................any of the branches of science dealing with matter and energy, often grouped into chemistry, physics, and Earth and space sciences

rocket engine...........................engine that propels a vehicle by the combustion of material and ejection of the gases produced

velocity......................................the speed and direction of an object over time

visualize ....to create a mental picture of

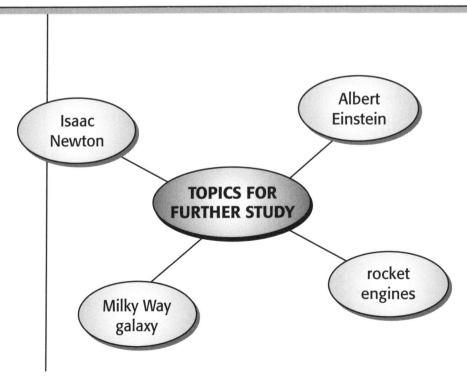

Bernouilli's Principle

Flowing Fluids

In 1738, Daniel Bernouilli described a physical principle that keeps airplanes aloft, rushes water through rapids, and can let us spray liquids without chemical pollutants. Bernouilli's principle explains that the pressure of a fluid decreases as its speed increases. How does that apply to the examples above? The following three activities will illustrate some of the effects of this fascinating scientific law.

Activity 1

To start, hold a strip of paper in front of your lower lip. Ask students what they think will happen if you blow across the top of the paper. (It will rise!) Encourage the students to try for themselves to test their predictions. Be sure not to blow air into others' faces.

Although we might predict that the air from our mouths will push the paper down, it actually draws it up. Faster-moving air over the top of the paper has lower internal pressure than the air underneath, which pushes the paper up. An airplane wing gets upward lift from the difference in the speed of the air along its top and bottom surfaces. This is fun to draw in a science notebook.

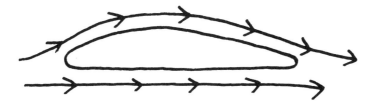

Activity 2

In the second activity, imagine a river narrowing down. The water must flow faster to keep the amount or volume of flow continuous. This is less surprising to us than the paper strip activity—the same amount of water flowing through a narrower passage must travel faster than it does through a wider passage. What's more surprising is that a moving flow of either water or air will pull things together.

To test Bernouilli's principle, fill a large container or tub with water. Have each team of students build two boats out of oaktag. Attach a string to each bow and drag them through the tub of water from opposite directions. The slower water on the outside of each ship pushes them toward each other. Ships passing in a narrow space must be careful not to crash broadside.

Have students discuss and diagram the currents—a clear container may serve as a wave tank with the water surface casting shadows on the bottom. Of course you must prepare for a wet activity, but the interesting physics should be worth it.

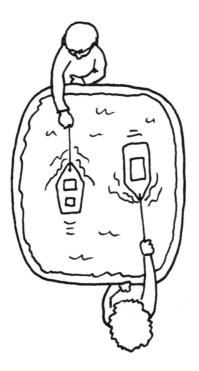

Activity 3

The third activity about Bernouilli's principle shows how to spray liquids without using chemical propellants. The method involves lowering the pressure over the liquid and giving it a path out of its container. Students can demonstrate this by making an atomizer.

Cut a straw so that part of it can be in a cup of water and part of it extends straight back toward you. When students blow air through the straw, water is drawn out of the cup and sprayed into the air.

Again, be sure not to blow water onto anyone! This activity works best outdoors.

Provide a pump spray mechanism for students to examine. It works by directing a faster flow of air, caused by the mechanical plunger, over a liquid. The flowing air picks up some of the liquid and delivers it as a spray. This can happen on a windy day at the beach. We might get wet even if we avoid the waves.

R E A D I N G:
Fluid Motion

Have you ever dropped sticks into the water and watched them float downstream? Their speed often varies greatly in different sections of the stream as the current changes. Some parts of rivers and streams are wide and lazy, while others are narrow and fast-moving.

Swiss scientist Daniel Bernouilli (1700–1782) may have gazed into many streams in his time. In 1738, Bernouilli described a physical principle that keeps airplanes aloft, rushes water through rapids, and can let us spray liquids without using chemical pollutants.

Bernouilli's principle explains that the pressure of a **fluid** decreases as its speed increases. It's fun to try experiments that illustrate this principle. Once you understand Bernouilli's discovery, you will find examples of it all around.

Think about examples of fluids flowing across the surfaces of objects. Spheres such as golf balls and baseballs curve because of unequal pressures as they spin. Extreme storm force winds blowing over a roof may lift it. A loose shower curtain can be drawn inward toward the flow of water.

Water rushing downstream (Courtesy of Christy Thompson, stock.xchng)

The gases swirling around a candle flame or air flowing past a spinning curve ball both behave the way they do because of **thermodynamics** and **aerodynamics.** *Thermo* means "heat," and *aero* means "flying." *Dynamics* means a lot of things, among them "moving" and "changing."

Daniel Bernouilli applied **calculus** to **physics** problems. Given a good formula and some data, it's amazing what people can do. Have you seen a plane fly by lately?

Vocabulary Words

aerodynamics	study of the interaction of atmospheric gases with moving objects
calculus	branch of mathematics dealing with rates of change and related concepts
fluid	substance that flows, usually but not always a gas or liquid
physics	branch of science concerned with the interaction between matter and energy
thermodynamics	study of the relationship between heat and other forms of energy

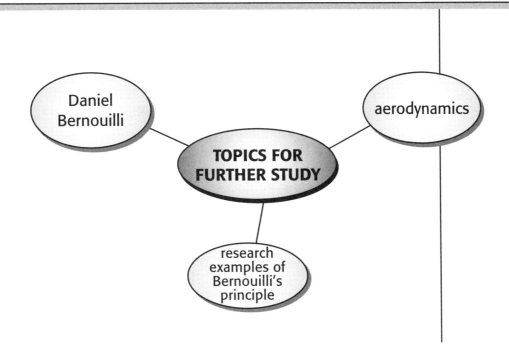

Materials per Team

- graph paper
- scissors
- buttons or other small objects

Relativity

Everything's Relative

Isaac Newton and the other pioneering scientists of the seventeenth century had a mental model of the "Clockwork Universe." Time flowed steadily and nature's laws could be calculated given enough logistical precision. Albert Einstein and the scientists of the twentieth century changed that view by including time in the category of variables. The passage of time is not the same for every situation. Position and movement affect the actual passage of time, not just the perception of time moving more slowly or quickly.

Most of these effects occur under conditions we do not experience in our everyday lives, such as speeds approaching the speed of light. However, understanding modern physics requires some understanding of relativity, and these activities will start students thinking that time is a measurement that can change.

Activity

To begin, have each group of students tape about four sheets of graph paper together end to end to make a simulated river. Using another sheet of graph paper, cut out a "boat" ten squares long and a few squares wide. Number the squares along the riverbank. Set up a chart to record the position of a passenger in the boat. Use a button or small marker to represent the passenger.

Time	Passenger Position Relative to Boat	Passenger Position Relative to Riverbank	Passenger Velocity Relative to Boat	Passenger Velocity Relative to Riverbank

Time	Boat Position Relative to Riverbank	Boat Velocity Relative to Riverbank

Explain velocity as the change in position from the previous recording, or change per time period. For simplicity, we will use standard time intervals of 10 seconds. The units in the table will be "squares per 10 seconds." Units for position will be "squares."

Place a button on the first square in the bow of the boat and start its trip down the river. Pretend the boat can move at a steady ten squares in 10 seconds. The passenger can also walk in the boat, taking 10 seconds to move one square. For the first simulated time period, move the boat ten squares downstream and move the button passenger one square toward the back of the boat.

Imagine an observer on the riverbank watching. In the first 10-second period, the boat has moved ten squares relative to the shoreline. The button has moved downstream only nine squares in 10 seconds, because the passenger walked toward the back of the boat while it was moving. The riverside observer would say the speed of the boat is ten squares per 10 seconds while the button's speed is nine squares per 10 seconds. To an observer on the boat, the button speed might be expressed as (-1) square per 10 seconds relative to the boat, because the passenger moved toward the back one square.

Starting Position at 0 Seconds

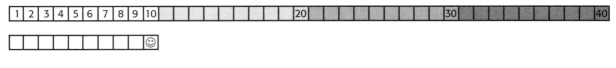

Position at 10 Seconds

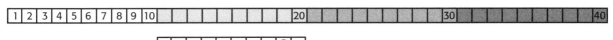

Time	Passenger Position Relative to Boat	Passenger Position Relative to Riverbank	Passenger Velocity Relative to Boat	Passenger Velocity Relative to Riverbank
0 seconds	0	0	no data	no data
10 seconds	-1	9	-1	9

Time	Boat Position Relative to Riverbank	Boat Velocity Relative to Riverbank
0 seconds	0	no data
10 seconds	10	10

Move the boat another ten squares and have the button stay in the same "seat" on the boat. Now the speeds of the button and the boat are the same relative to the riverbank. The boat has moved its constant ten squares and this time the button has also advanced ten squares. An observer in the boat could remark that the button did not move relative to the boat.

Time	Passenger Position Relative to Boat	Passenger Position Relative to Riverbank	Passenger Velocity Relative to Boat	Passenger Velocity Relative to Riverbank
0 seconds	0	0	no data	no data
10 seconds	-1	9	-1	9
20 seconds	0	19	0	10

Time	Boat Position Relative to Riverbank	Boat Velocity Relative to Riverbank
0 seconds	0	no data
10 seconds	10	10
20 seconds	20	10

Finally, move the boat another ten squares, and move the button one square forward in the boat. Over this 10-second interval, the shore observer sees the boat move its steady ten squares in 10 seconds, while the button has advanced its position eleven squares. Within the boat, the button passenger has moved one square forward in 10 seconds, while the boat itself has advanced ten squares as measured from the riverbank.

Time	Passenger Position Relative to Boat	Passenger Position Relative to Riverbank	Passenger Velocity Relative to Boat	Passenger Velocity Relative to Riverbank
0 seconds	0	0	no data	no data
10 seconds	-1	9	-1	9
20 seconds	0	19	0	10
30 seconds	1	30	1	11

Time	Boat Position Relative to Riverbank	Boat Velocity Relative to Riverbank
0 seconds	0	no data
10 seconds	10	10
20 seconds	20	10
30 seconds	30	10

All of these speeds are relative. Einstein theorized that space and time are relative. That means both position and motion are perceived according to where the observer is. The speed of light, however, is an absolute and remains constant to all observers.

Position in the universe can be expressed by three dimensions of space (roughly up and down, back and forth, and side to side) and a fourth dimension of time. Describing motion depends on the frame of reference of the observer. Whether the observer and the mover are in the same compartment or have different perspectives makes a lot of difference. In our example in this activity, passengers on a boat compare their movements to each other's positions in the cabin. They could play catch on the boat. Because they are both moving together, it would seem as if they are standing still and only the ball is moving.

As students advance into studying Einstein and his famous theories, they will learn that time is relative, too. The famous formula, $E = mc^2$, uses the speed of light (c) as a mathematical link between energy and mass because the value remains constant.

READING:

Standing on Newton's Shoulders

Isaac Newton's (1642–1727) laws of motion have been studied since he formulated them in the seventeenth century. Newton's view of the universe might be compared to the insides of a wind-up clock. Time ticks along steadily, gears turn, objects sweep along in graceful **arcs,** and everything is understandable if observed and measured carefully.

In the twentieth century, a new set of rules about motion was proposed by Albert Einstein (1879–1955). Einstein theorized that all motion is relative. It can only be described in comparison to the motion of another object. Einstein explained that because motion may be measured by change of position over time, time itself is relative.

When we sit still, our bodies are actually in quite a bit of motion. We ride the spinning Earth, which travels around the sun. The sun is moving through space, bringing the entire solar system with it. Our local group of stars, the **Milky Way** galaxy, moves relative to other **galaxies.** Newton's laws work well on Earth for the most part and are still very useful. Einstein's ideas have helped people understand motion on both very small and very large scales.

Albert Einstein did not do well in school as a youth. But he was interested in physics and especially the nature of **waves.** He was fascinated by **magnets.** The attracting power of a magnet is invisible but can be strong. Earlier in the nineteenth century, during a time of great advances in physics, others were exploring invisible forces.

▶ Michael Faraday (1791–1867) explained how **electricity** and magnetism were connected.

▶ James Maxwell (1831–1879) named the force **electromagnetic** waves. Maxwell created mathematical equations to describe the behavior of waves.

Force fields were discovered to be around sources of electromagnetic waves. Einstein built on this knowledge and reasoned that objects would have **gravity** force fields around them too.

According to Einstein's theories, time is not a constant. Time will vary according to speed, so space and time are connected. An object's length and mass will change depending upon its velocity, but these will not change significantly until extremely high speeds. The only absolute, unchanging value in the universe is the **speed of light.**

Another great leap of understanding made by Albert Einstein was the linking of matter and energy. His famous equation $E = mc^2$ means that energy is equal to mass times the speed of light (c) squared. The speed of light is already a large number and *squared* means "multiply it times itself." So even a tiny amount of mass can produce a huge amount of energy. When scientists succeeded in splitting an atom, powerful amounts of nuclear energy were produced.

All the great changes in the study of physics have been revolutionary. People have had to abandon ideas that were held for centuries in favor of theories that fit the facts more completely. Proof of some of Einstein's ideas had to wait for the development of technology to test them.

What discoveries will the future of physics bring? Learning more about the very small (**subatomic particles**) and the very large (distant objects in the universe) may hold the key to why matter and energy behave as they do.

Albert Einstein

Vocabulary Words

arc.. segment of a curve

electricity .... the force caused by the attraction between unlike charges and the repulsion between like forces

electromagnetism.................. type of radiation that travels in the form of waves

galaxy.. group of stars orbiting a common center. Galaxies also contain gas, dust, and solid objects.

gravity.. force of attraction between objects based on their mass

magnet... an object that attracts substances containing certain metals, especially iron

Milky Way .... spiral galaxy containing our solar system

speed of light......................... approximately 300,000 kilometers per second (186,000 miles per second) in a vacuum

subatomic particles.............. the components of atoms, any form of matter smaller than the atom itself

waves... energy that travels across space as motion or disturbance

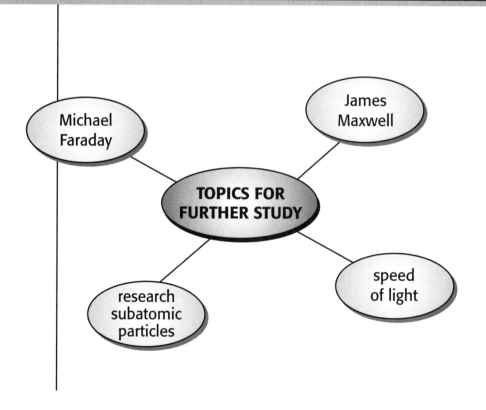

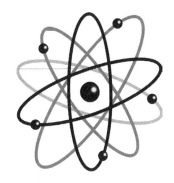

CHAPTER 2

Chemistry

TIME LINE

Year	Notable Event
460 B.C.	Democritus of Greece named smallest bits of matter atoms.
1620	Jan Baptista van Helmont invented the term *gas.*
1662	Robert Boyle experimented with gases at different temperatures and pressures.
1766	Henry Cavendish produced hydrogen and oxygen from water.
1772	Joseph Priestley experimented with air, identifying and separating several of its components.
1778	Antoine Lavoisier identified one gas as about 25% of air and another as about 75%. We now call these *oxygen* and *nitrogen.*
1803	John Dalton explained his atomic theory.
1827	Robert Brown observed that particles in a liquid are constantly in motion.
1869	Dmitri Mendeleyev created a periodic table of elements.
1895	Wilhelm Roentgen discovered X rays.
1896	Antoine-Henri Becquerel described radioactivity.
1905	Albert Einstein described Brownian motion as the continuous movement of particles.
1911	Marie Curie won a Nobel Prize for discovering radium and polonium.
1911	Ernest Rutherford described the structure of an atom as consisting of a nucleus and electrons.
1913	Henry Moseley announced his findings about the atomic number of elements, stating that elements have a constant number of protons and electrons.
1923	Johannes Bronsted and Thomas Lowry independently described the role of ions in acids and bases.
1942	Enrico Fermi produced a sustained nuclear reaction.

Materials per Team

- sand
- salt
- water
- measuring cups or graduated cylinders
- magnifying lenses
- plastic straws or medicine droppers
- string
- scissors

Solutions and Mixtures

Will It Dissolve?

The action of chemistry occurs on the molecular level but we see things on a much larger scale. From our modern vantage point, we know a lot about atoms and molecules. Provide students with an opportunity to experiment and then help them think through how molecules behave. Then they can build their own theoretical understanding of the mechanism of chemistry.

Activity

Open the activity by looking at some salt and sand with magnifying lenses and microscopes. The salt cubes and the variety of small bits of sand are examples of crystals, regularly shaped pieces with flat surfaces. The sand is weathered and not as regular but its crystalline structure should be apparent when magnified.

Have students from each team fill two containers with equal amounts of warm water. Two hundred milliliters (mL) works well. Next, tell them to add a measured volume of salt (10 to 20 mL) to one cup and an identical amount of sand to the other. They should determine if the volume of water in the cups changes measurably. They can then stir the liquids and notice how the salt dissolves and forms a solution while the sand simply settles out after spending some time as a mixture.

Have students use two different straws to draw up some of the water. They should never suck liquid up the straw with their mouths during science experiments—instead, tell them to simply dip the straw in the water and place a finger on the top end. Place a few drops from each cup on plates or trays. Tell them to observe what happens as the water evaporates. Have them examine the resulting salt crystal with the magnifying lens. The water from the sand mixture should leave no residue if the mixture has had time to settle out and the sand had sunk to the bottom.

Tell students to cut the straws so that they will lie across the top of the mixing containers. Then they can tie a string to each straw and let the string sink into the mixture. They may need to use a "sinker" to keep the string from floating. (A paper clip works well and may rust in the water, leading to the "Taking Oxygen Out of the Air" activity on page 61, "Iron + Oxygen = Rust.") To avoid rust at this point, have students use a sinker made of a material other than metal. Put the containers in a spot where they won't be disturbed and can be easily observed over a few days.

The salt and water combined to form a solution. The sand and water mixed but neither material changed. They remained separate. The "Atomic Bonds" activity on page 52 uses model building to simulate this process.

R E A D I N G:

Atoms, Compounds, and Solutions

Since ancient times people have wondered about the structure of matter. Democritus (c. 460–370 B.C.), a Greek scientist from the fifth century B.C., theorized that a substance could be reduced to smaller and smaller bits until eventually what you had were atoms. Atoms would be the smallest pieces of a substance and could not be divided further.

Other theories, which lasted into the 1800s, claimed that all matter was made up of earth, air, fire, and water. These "elements" supposedly combined in different ways to make everything else.

Both sand and salt are **minerals** from the Earth that form **crystals.** Look at them closely with a magnifying lens and you will see the salt as regularly shaped pieces with flat surfaces. The sand is weathered and not so regular but its **crystalline** structure should be apparent when magnified.

These materials behave very differently from each other in water. Water, sand, and salt are **compounds,** substances made up of more than one type of **atom** bonded together. English chemist John Dalton (1766–1844) proposed an atomic theory of matter in 1803. Dalton explained that **elements** are substances consisting of only one kind of atom. Atoms combine to form larger quantities of elements, and atoms from two or more elements can combine to form compounds. Because chemicals mix in exact proportions, Dalton reasoned that atoms of each element must be combining with atoms of other elements.

Crystal formation

Salt and water will combine to form a **solution.** The sand and water can mix, but neither material changes and they remain separate. What other compounds do you know? Very few elements exist in a pure state in nature.

As you do chemical experiments and make models of atoms and molecules, imagine how clever scientists were to figure out these structures. Much science is based on careful observation, and then our brains must take over and reason with the data.

Vocabulary Words

atom .... the smallest unit of an element

compound .... in chemistry, a substance made up of the atoms of two or more elements bonded into molecules

crystal .... arrangement of matter in which the molecules are aligned in a regular, repeating structure

crystalline .... relating to crystal structure

element...................................... substance composed of one type of atom

mineral...................................... naturally occurring inorganic (not from living things) solid substance with a specific chemical composition and crystal structure

solution.................................... evenly distributed mixture of two or more substances

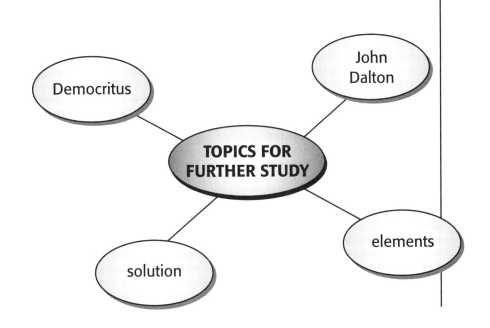

Materials per Team

- tennis balls (three per group)
- golf or Ping Pong balls (two per group)
- marbles or other small objects (38 per group)
- marking pens
- construction paper or oaktag
- paper fasteners
- scissors
- hole punch
- Periodic Table of the Elements chart

Atomic Bonds

Making Atomic Models

Understanding the way things behave on the molecular level opens up a unique perspective on the world. We see the reactions and can imagine how the molecules interact. How can students grasp the concepts of atomic structure? Making models with common materials can help.

Models can illustrate the difference between two basic ways atoms combine to form molecules—ionic and covalent bonds. The atomic bonds activities present simple ways to simulate these interactions among atoms and help students begin to understand the structure of the periodic table. The first activity uses spheres and the second uses paper and fasteners.

Activity 1

Ask students to recall the activity with water, salt, and sand as a discussion starter. (See the "Solutions and Mixtures" activity on page 48.) One powder dissolved while the other didn't. The water and salt molecules interacted and because of the way their atoms are bonded, the water dissolved the salt.

Salt is composed of sodium (Na) and chlorine (Cl) atoms in equal proportion. Water molecules consist of structures made of two hydrogen (H) atoms for each oxygen (O) atom. Sand is composed of the worn-down parts of rock and shell. Quartz is a major mineral component of sand and is formed by the elements silicon (Si) and oxygen.

Use golf or Ping Pong balls to represent the nuclei of hydrogen atoms and use tennis balls for the others. Atoms of the same element always have the same number of protons in their nucleus. This is called the *atomic number,* and it places the element on the periodic table. For this exercise, each group will need two hydrogen nuclei (Ping Pong balls) and three tennis balls (one each for oxygen, sodium, and chlorine).

Write the chemical symbol and atomic number on the balls with a marking pen. Emphasize that the number tells how many protons are contained in the nucleus. Groups of students can find the atomic numbers independently (H = 1, O = 16, Na = 11, and Cl = 17). The Periodic Table of the Elements is arranged in order by atomic number. Be sure students understand that atoms of different elements have different-sized nuclei. However, in this simulation we are using only two sizes and they are not to scale.

The marbles or other small objects represent the electrons. Each individual atom has the same number of electrons as there are protons in its nucleus. Atoms usually do not exist in nature as individual entities. They are so highly reactive that most are bound up in compounds. It is the interaction of the electrons that create bonds between atoms.

Electrons create a series of shells around the nucleus of the atom. Each shell has a specific capacity of electrons it can hold. The first shell can hold two, the second shell can hold eight, and the third can also hold eight.

Teams of students can build models of the atoms that compose the compounds water and salt following those patterns. Use a tennis ball for each atom's nucleus and place the marbles in concentric rings to represent electrons.

For example, a sodium chloride (salt) molecule consists of structures made with sodium atoms and chlorine atoms. Sodium atoms have an atomic number of 11. Each sodium atom model needs a tennis ball nucleus marked "Na 11," two marbles in the first ring, eight in the second, and only one in the outer ring.

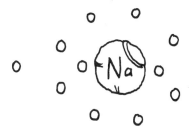

Use chlorine as another example. It has an atomic number of 17. Challenge students to assemble a model chlorine atom. It should have a tennis ball nucleus marked "Cl 17," surrounded by rings containing two, eight, and seven marbles.

When their outer shells are below full capacity, atoms will seek to combine with other atoms to complete their shells. Because the chlorine atom needs only one electron to fill its outer shell, and the sodium atom has only one in its outer shell, the two atoms bond together. The lone electron moves from the sodium to the chlorine atom's shell. Both atoms now have outer shells containing eight electrons.

But the match between their protons and electrons is thrown off. The chlorine atom now has more electrons than protons, giving it a negative charge. The sodium atom is positively charged, because it has more protons. Atoms or groups of atoms with an overall electrical charge like these are called *ions.* This kind of bond is called an *ionic bond.*

Water forms a different kind of bond. Hydrogen has an atomic number of 1 while oxygen is element number 8. Using the tennis balls and marbles again, have students construct an oxygen atom. Oxygen has a filled inner shell of two and an outer shell of six electrons, which is two short of full. Construct two hydrogen atoms with smaller nuclei and only one electron each.

Instead of the oxygen borrowing the two electrons from the hydrogen atoms, the three atoms share the electrons. The electrons travel around all the nuclei. This kind of bond is called a covalent bond. The atoms still have positive or negative charges but electrons are "lost" or "gained" temporarily instead of being on permanent loan.

How do the two compounds the students modeled interact with each other?

When salt dissolves in water, the sodium ion with its positive charge is attracted to the negatively charged oxygen atom. The negatively charged chlorine ion is attracted to the positively charged hydrogen. Because hydrogen and oxygen are tightly bonded and share electrons, the H_2O does not break up. But the Na and Cl can be pulled apart and dissolved by the water, which breaks the ionic bond holding the salt together.

As the water evaporates, the sodium and chlorine are once again attracted to each other and reform into crystals.

Why doesn't the sand dissolve in water? The covalent bonds in sand between the silicon atoms and oxygen atoms are very strong. The silicon already has oxygen atoms as partners and therefore does not "need" the oxygen from the water to fill its outer shell.

Activity 2

To demonstrate ionic and covalent bonding another way, have students cut out circles from strong paper to represent each atom. Tell them to draw a small inner circle as the nucleus, labeling it with the chemical symbol and atomic number for each atom. To show electrons, draw concentric outer rings and color an appropriate number of dots to represent each filled shell. When they reach the outermost ring, students should punch the number of holes to show its capacity. For each electron the atom actually has in the outer ring, they will fill one hole with a paper fastener.

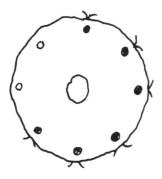

Atoms are very reactive and want to keep their outer electron shells filled. Have students remove the Na's single fastener and place it into the one empty space in the outer ring of the Cl atom. The Na "donates" its lone outer electron to the Cl, satisfying the need to have filled outer shells. But because the atoms now have different numbers of protons and electrons, they become charged ions and tightly bonded to each other.

Students can construct the covalent water molecule by putting the fasteners through the holes of both the H and O atoms. Students might think of this bond as sharing rather than loaning. Try making other compounds with this method and the periodic table. For example, both oxygen gas molecules and hydrogen gas molecules consist of a pair of atoms bonding.

Models are imperfect but are meant to be helpful. Remind students that these activities are designed to demonstrate the style of bond, not present an actual picture.

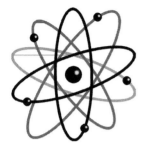

READING:
Atomic Bonds

People have thought about atoms since at least the time of the ancient Greeks. Constructing models of atoms has been an ongoing task. Atoms are too small to be seen by our eyes, even when using conventional **light-gathering microscopes.** Scientists have had to use deductive reasoning, **electron scanning microscopes,** collisions that smash atoms into smaller particles, and other means to build a picture of an atom. By studying the behavior of different materials, scientists steadily gained a better idea of how atoms might look.

Up to the eighteenth century, most scientists believed atoms to be indivisible (unable to be broken). Even though atoms couldn't be seen, they were probably pictured as being tiny copies of the larger bits of matter that were visible. John Dalton's (1766–1844) conclusions about atoms were more scientific.

Dalton and other experimenters separated material into **elements.** Elements are substances consisting of only one kind of atom. Atoms combine to form larger quantities of elements, and atoms from two or more elements combine to form **compounds.**

Scientists in the 1700s learned about gases and their properties. Robert Brown (1773–1858) also made his important finding that molecules (particles made from atoms bonded together) are always moving.

When more elements were identified, they could be sorted into categories. That paved the way for major breakthroughs in the discovery of atomic structure. Dmitri Mendeleev (1834–1907) organized elements by their properties and masses. He listed them in a chart aligned according to atomic weight, now called **atomic mass.** Mendeleev was able to predict the existence of undiscovered elements based on his **Periodic Table of the Elements.**

In 1911, Ernest Rutherford (1871–1937) was able to pass some particles through a super thin sheet of gold while others bounced off. He reasoned that most of the mass of an atom must be concentrated in a central **nucleus** surrounded by **electrons.** The particles bouncing back were striking the nucleus of an atom. Two years later, Neils Bohr (1885–1962) described electrons as moving in definite orbital layers. When an electron changes its orbit, energy is either released or absorbed. The release of energy occurs in a specific bundle, or **quantum,** of energy.

Joseph John Thomson (1856–1940) applied **electric current** between two metal plates in a **vacuum tube** and produced a stream of electrons. No matter which metal or gas he sealed into the tube, the particle stream traveled from the positive plate to the negative plate with the same properties.

The dense nucleus was found to contain **protons** (positively charged) and **neutrons** (no electrical charge), which in turn are composed of smaller units. Outside the nucleus, electrons carry a negative electrical charge. The number of protons in the nucleus of an element remains constant, as Henry Moseley (1887–1915) announced in 1913. The number of neutrons can change, producing **isotopes,** or atoms of the same element with a different mass.

The key to the periodic table turned out to be the arrangement of electrons in the individual atoms. Each electron layer forms a sort of a cloud. Imagine a fan turning so fast that you do not see the individual blades. Instead, a sort of shell is formed. Rutherford imagined the atom in some ways as a tiny copy of the solar system. But planets tend to stay in a narrow plane and follow a defined path around the sun. Electrons take up an area closer to the shape of a **sphere.**

Each orbital layer can hold a maximum number of electrons at any one time. When the outermost layer is "full," the atom is very stable and unlikely to react with other atoms. Reactions between atoms occur when the outer layers of electrons combine and the orbits reach full occupancy.

As the twentieth century began, experimenters worked with particles on smaller and smaller levels. Scientists found that some elements emitted **radiation,** or waves of energy. Antoine Becquerel (1852–1908) found that uranium compounds gave off rays that would penetrate many solid objects. Marie Curie (1867–1934), the first person to win two **Nobel Prizes,** and her husband Pierre Curie (1859–1906) helped isolate the element radium. That discovery further explained the emission of **radioactivity.**

Scientists continue to search for smaller **subatomic particles** that make up the atom. Electrons sometimes behave like **waves** and sometimes like **particles.** We may not be able to draw or build a model atom to reflect that **paradox.**

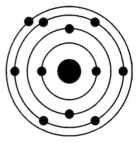

Illustration of a sodium atom

Vocabulary Words

atomic mass .... number of protons and neutrons in an atom's nucleus. Each individual atom's mass is a whole number, but because of isotopes, the average atomic mass for any element may be expressed as a decimal.

compound .... in chemistry, a substance made up of the atoms of two or more elements bonded into molecules

electric current .... flow of an electrical charge

electron scanning
microscope .... device in which a beam of electrons contacts a specimen and creates a highly magnified image of it

electrons .... negatively charged particles in the shell around the nucleus of an atom

element .... substance composed of one type of atom

isotopes .... atoms of the same element containing different numbers of neutrons

light-gathering
microscope .... optical device used for magnifying small objects by refracting light through the use of lenses

neutrons .... subatomic particle in the nucleus carrying no electrical charge

Nobel Prize .... international prize awarded for outstanding achievement in a variety of fields

nucleus .... in a cell, the part separated by a membrane and containing most of the cell's DNA. In an atom, a positively charged mass containing protons and neutrons.

paradox .... a contradiction, often occurring when two statements appear to be true alone but seem to disagree when considered together

particles .... tiny pieces; minute parts

Periodic Table
of the Elements .... a chart organizing the elements by atomic structure and chemical properties

protons .... subatomic particle in the nucleus carrying a positive electrical charge

Vocabulary Words *(continued)*

quantum...................................a unit of a quantity that operates as a discrete bundle. Quantum theory states that energy radiates in "packages" of specific amounts.

radiation ....energy emission by means of waves or particles

radioactivity ....process in which an element breaks apart or decays to become another element, emitting high-frequency waves

sphere ....solid round figure

subatomic particles...............the components of atoms, any form of matter smaller than the atom itself

vacuum tube ....a sealed tube in an electronic device through which electrons flow

waves.......................................energy that travels across space as motion or disturbance

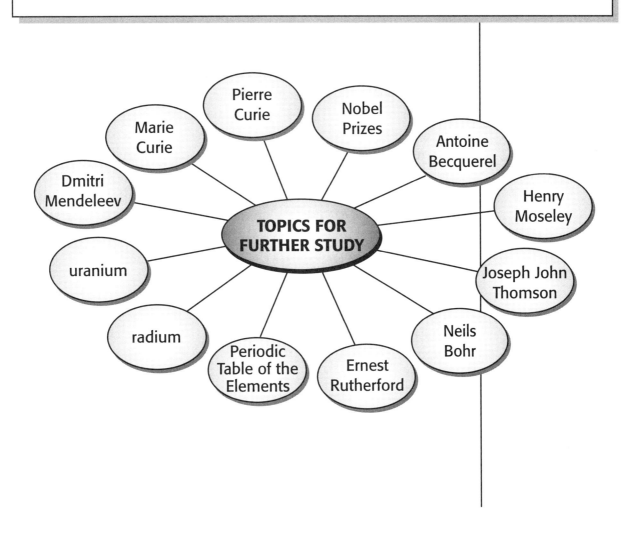

Materials per Team

- vinegar
- baking soda
- cups
- spoons
- small candle, safely set within a glass of water

Solid, Liquid, and Gas

Solid + Liquid = Gas

Matter generally occurs in three states: solid, liquid, and gas. Students will be familiar with water as a common substance that they've experienced in each form. Ice is solid, or crystallized, water. They will know that liquid water disappears, or evaporates, when left uncovered. The gas, called *water vapor*, is invisible. The "steam" we see emanating from a boiling kettle is composed of water droplets, many of which do become vapor and mix with the air.

Activity

In this activity, students will combine a solid (baking soda) and a liquid (vinegar) to form a gas (carbon dioxide). Start with equal volumes of chemicals and have students combine them by pouring vinegar into the baking soda. Then students can experiment with different amounts of each component and compare the reactions. Does it make a difference if the ratio is two to one, vinegar to baking soda, versus the opposite way? Does it matter if you add the baking soda to vinegar versus adding vinegar to baking soda? (The resulting mixture from this experiment is safe to go down the sink.) Allow plenty of time for this exciting activity, and be sure to work over trays and newspaper.

When the gas produced by this reaction is poured onto a lit candle, the flame goes out. You can show this as a demonstration. The carbon dioxide (CO_2) extinguishes the flame by denying it oxygen (O_2). The CO_2 is more dense than the air and displaces it, depriving the candle of the O_2 it needs to continue burning.

Some fire extinguishers work on a similar principle. When a chemical reaction is created, the foam, with its non-flammable gas, is sprayed onto the fire. Without O_2 to fuel the combustion process, the fire goes out.

Taking Oxygen Out of the Air

Iron + Oxygen = Rust

Chemical reactions occur on the molecular level but the results can sometimes be observed. Rust results when oxygen combine with iron. In this activity, students will observe this process.

Materials per Team

- steel wool, without soap
- three test tubes or thin vials
- wide transparent cups or saucers
- water
- bleach and vinegar (optional, and especially for older students)

Activity

Have students dampen some steel wool and stuff it into the bottom of a test tube or thin vial. Use steel wool that is manufactured for polishing, not the type that contains soap. In another tube, have them stuff in dry steel wool. Ask them to be sure the steel wool won't fall out when the tubes are inverted. Place those two tubes, along with an empty tube, mouth down in a wide cup or saucer filled partway with water.

Have students carefully observe the test tubes over the next few days. The damp steel wool rusts as the iron (a component of steel) combines with oxygen, forming iron oxide. Because oxygen is drawn from the air for this chemical reaction, the volume of air in the test tube is reduced and water rises up into it. The water levels in the other tubes do not rise as there is no chemical reaction involving oxygen.

An acid solution will make iron rust even faster. To show this, mix two parts of bleach to one part vinegar. Do this as a demonstration, and do not get this on you, as it creates an acid solution (hydrochloric acid, HClO). Once they add steel wool to the mixture, rusting begins quickly.

READING:

▶ *SOLID, LIQUID AND GAS*

▶ *TAKING OXYGEN OUT OF THE AIR*

Discovering How Things Burn

What happens when things burn? This question puzzled chemists (and everyone else) before the 1800s. Materials need air to burn—that was discovered pretty easily. But why, and what is the chemical process that occurs?

Air baffled and fascinated scientists for much of the history of chemistry. Robert Boyle (1627–1691) learned that air is necessary for fire and for animals to breathe. He also theorized that elements are substances that cannot be broken down into other substances.

A Belgian scientist named Jan Baptista van Helmont (1579–1644) invented the term *gas* from a word meaning "chaos." Van Helmont studied how things burned and discovered that there were different kinds of gases.

Early **alchemists** had learned how to make **calx.** *Calx* was their term for a powdery substance that some metals formed when heated. Although alchemists made important discoveries, many of them were dishonest. They tried to fool people into thinking they knew how to make gold.

Boyle thought that fire itself had weight, which became added to the metal when calx formed. After all, the calx was heavier than the original metal. Georg Ernst Stahl (1660–1734) theorized that there was a substance in flammable materials called **phlogiston.** Stahl thought the phlogiston escaped when objects burned or metals formed calx. But it didn't make sense that the calx weighed more than the original material.

The phlogiston theory was wrong but was accepted for many years. More discoveries about gas and air led to its replacement. Joseph Black (1728–1799) explained that some gases are not air. Joseph Priestly (1733–1804) was able to separate oxygen from air and called it "de-phlogisticated air." Priestly learned that plants could restore air that had been used for burning. Henry Cavendish (1731–1810) collected the element hydrogen from a chemical reaction, calling it **inflammable** air. Cavendish also was among the first scientists to weigh gases.

Antoine Lavoisier (1743–1794) found that matter combines with oxygen, one of the gases in air, when it burns. Air is not an element, Lavoisier and others discovered, but is made up of a mixture of gases. He was able to break it down into two gases. Even when a chemical change occurs, such as burning, the mass of matter stays the same.

Lavoisier figured out that when things burn, they combine with oxygen from the air. When the oxygen is gone, the fire goes out.

Rust is a slower version of the process of burning. When things rust, iron combines with oxygen and forms a reddish compound called *iron oxide.* Fire and rust, like many chemical mysteries, can be explained by the reactions caused when atoms and molecules interact.

Rusty chain (Courtesy of Neil Gould, stock.xchng)

Vocabulary Words

alchemist .... name for medieval chemists, some of whom claimed or sought the ability to turn other metals into gold

calx .... crumbly residue produced by a chemical change when a mineral or metal has been heated

inflammable .... catches fire easily

phlogiston .... non-existent substance that early chemists mistakenly believed to be released in the form of flame when things burned

rust .... scaly result of iron combining with oxygen

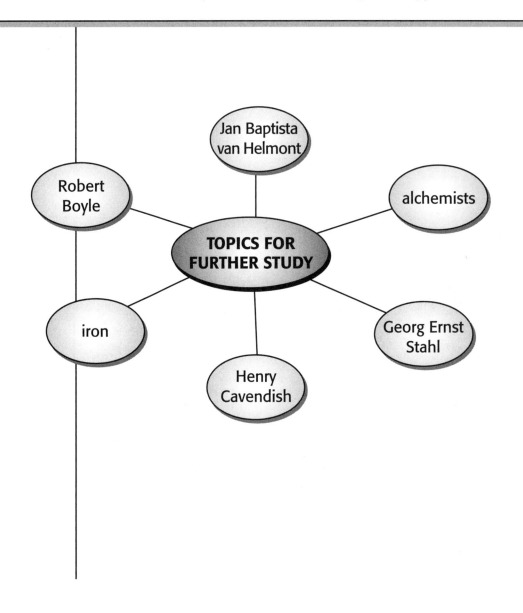

Brownian Motion

Diffusion

From *Science Giants: Physical Science* © Good Year Books. This page may be reproduced for classroom use only by the actual purchaser of the book. www.goodyearbooks.com

In 1827 Robert Brown observed pollen grains in a liquid under a microscope. The grains moved in jumpy, random motions. Observing other tiny particles that were obviously not alive, Brown also saw them move and reasoned that something was happening on a very small scale. We now attribute that movement to the continuous motion of molecules, the building blocks of all substances. The collisions between molecules (both those of the fluid and the solid) changed the direction of the motion. This movement is called *Brownian motion.*

Materials per Team

- food color
- water
- measuring devices (spoons, graduated cylinders or test tubes, etc.)
- 1-liter soft drink bottles

Activity

The process of diffusion, the gradual mixing of two gases or fluids, is related to Brownian motion. When diffusion occurs, molecules travel from an area where they are highly concentrated to an area of lower concentration.

This activity helps students visualize and understand three concepts. It simulates Brownian motion, demonstrates diffusion, and allows students to control the concentration of a mixture by diluting it.

To begin, provide each team with several clean 1-liter soft drink containers. Have students fill one with plain water at room temperature. They can measure as they fill to be sure each bottle holds 1000 milliliters (mL) of water. Tell them to add a drop of food color (also at room temperature) to the container and observe how the color spreads gradually to all parts of the container.

On a molecular level, many collisions between water molecules cause the movement of the color. The principle of diffusion explains the even spread of the color. Have them continue to add drops until they have a dark, evenly colored liquid. Have them cap and shake the bottle to speed up mixing as necessary.

Your students have 1000 mL of a colored liquid solution. Call this Solution 1. Instruct teams to dilute Solution 1 with fresh water to 10% of its concentration. They will need to measure and pour 100 mL into another container and then add enough plain water (900 mL) to bring this up to 1000 mL. Drawing diagrams of this process in a science notebook helps clarify the recording. Call the dilution Solution 2.

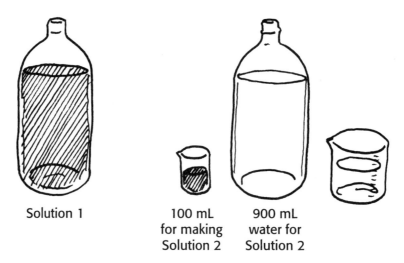

Solution 1   100 mL for making Solution 2   900 mL water for Solution 2

Tell students to repeat the dilution process, making 10% solutions until the resulting liquid finally appears clear. How many times must they dilute the liquid until they no longer see color? Have students predict how many dilutions will be necessary.

It is a surprisingly low number so you won't need to be gathering bottles forever! Don't give away the activity before students try it, but plan to have at least five bottles per team. If you can't obtain a supply of bottles, large transparent cups will work, but you will have to reduce all the volumes. For large transparent cups, measure the original amount to 200 mL and remove 20 mL for each successive dilution.

Discuss the relationship between pollution and dilution. If water is added to a pollutant, does it go away quickly? What does it mean when concentrations are given in parts per million? Have students use some or all of the representations in the chart in their notebooks to reinforce the concept of dilution.

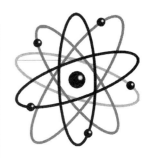

READING:
Molecules in Motion

Things are not always what they appear to be. A desk or a table seems absolutely solid, and that is just what we call that form of matter—solid. After all, it is not a liquid or a gas.

But the more scientists learned about the behavior of atoms and molecules, the less solid things seemed. There is mostly space in atoms, but the forces holding them together are so strong that they can behave like **solids.** Under different conditions, matter can also take the form of a **liquid** or **gas.** Substances can change form because of heat, pressure, and other forces.

Many different discoveries about gases and liquids led to the modern model of the atom. Most of the mass of an atom is in a tiny nucleus. Shell-like layers of orbiting electrons surround the nucleus. Because these parts could not be seen, a lot of clever thinking and hard work has led to modern ideas about what atoms look like.

Robert Brown (1773–1858) observed **pollen** grains in a liquid under a microscope in 1827. The grains moved in jumpy, random motions. At first, Brown thought the grains were alive. But he saw similar movement in other tiny particles that he knew were not alive. Brown reasoned that something was happening at a very small scale. He could not explain the reason.

In 1905, Albert Einstein (1879–1955) explained "Brownian motion" as the result of the continuous motion of **molecules.** Molecules are composed of atoms strongly bonded together and are the building blocks of all substances. The collisions between molecules (both those of the liquid and the floating solid grains) caused changes in the direction of the motion.

Diffusion is the name for the gradual mixing of two gases or fluids. It is related to Brownian motion. When diffusion occurs, molecules travel from an area where they are highly concentrated (many close together) to an area of lower concentration.

Even in solids, molecules are always moving, although they can be very tightly bonded together. The reason our desks and tables are so solid is because the molecules of wood or other material are rigidly connected to each other. Molecules in liquids have less sturdy connections, and gas molecules travel quite freely. In any form, matter is composed mostly of empty space.

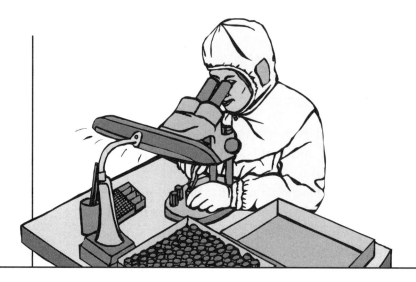

Vocabulary Words

diffusion...................................... gradual mixing of molecules due to random motion

gas.. state of matter in which molecules have no definite shape and fill whatever space is available

liquid.. state of matter having definite volume but taking the shape of the container in which it is confined

molecule...................................... two or more atoms bonded together

pollen .... material produced by anthers of flowers that is the male element in fertilization

solid .... state of matter having definite shape and volume

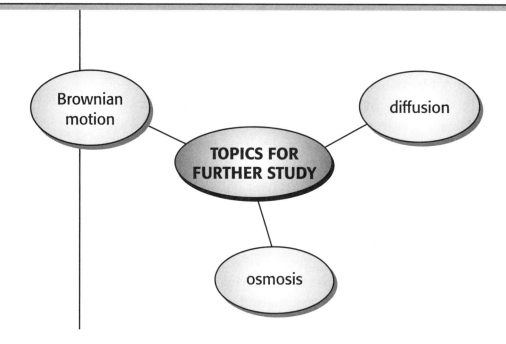

Brownian motion

diffusion

TOPICS FOR FURTHER STUDY

osmosis

From *Science Giants: Physical Science* © Good Year Books. This page may be reproduced for classroom use only by the actual purchaser of the book. www.goodyearbooks.com

Search for the Perfect Mess

The Search for the Perfect Mess

Chemistry appeals to students for many reasons. It's messy, there's an element of trial and error, and some of the outcomes are surprising. Many technological achievements occurred because of accidental or serendipitous chemical discoveries. Here's a chance for students to experience the satisfaction of developing their own formulas. The activity can be messy, but the opportunities for learning abound and the materials are common and benign. Under adult supervision, the activities can be repeated or extended at home.

Note: *Because of the probability of sloppy lab tables, put down plenty of newspaper and forewarn students to wear work clothes. Keep science notebooks away from the experiments.*

Materials per Team

- two large containers, one each for corn starch and water
- two small vials (film canisters, medicine cups, etc.) for measuring
- small disposable cups, one per student for mixing
- mixing spoon or stick

Activity

After distributing materials, ask students to use the small vials to measure one container of water and one of corn starch. Have them mix the materials together in a small paper cup. What does the resulting mixture look and feel like? Make sure students note their observations on their lab charts.

Note: *Do not dispose of materials down the drain. Wrap them in newspaper and dispose in the trash.*

Corn Starch	Water	Results
1	1	soupy white liquid
2	1	?
3	2	?

Suggest that the classroom chemists find a recipe that produces a substance kids will enjoy. What proportion of cornstarch to water produces a pleasing mixture to touch? In addition to careful recording, sharing results among groups will help students feel as if they are part of an R&D (Research and Development) Team. When a group discovers an entertaining combination, everyone will know!

Cornstarch mixtures are easier to clean when dry. The crumbly powder can be vacuumed or swept up.

Note: *Do not put this material down a drain, as it may harden and block the drain.*

Try to involve students in the clean-up process. Not only will your burden of work be lighter, but the mixture's interesting behavior continues as it dries.

You can follow up the lab with a language activity about advertising. How would they market the mixture so it would appeal to consumers? Adding food color to the water creates colorful slimy material, and a catchy name, logo, or advertising slogan could build product recognition. Posters, commercial skits, mail-order brochures, and other marketing tactics can provide a rich experience. Once the students begin to brainstorm the possible components of an ad campaign, the list of potential activities will grow quickly. Maybe a class of younger students can be a test group of consumers.

The material itself has many interesting properties, several of which should be central to the ad campaign. The substance students will like best flows as if it is liquid, but when compressed it feels like a solid. The warmth of a hand seems to reduce its viscosity (resistance to movement) but applying pressure by squeezing makes it stiff.

What other attributes can students describe? The mixture is a non-Newtonian fluid. Generally, in this type of non-Newtonian fluid, the viscosity is affected by pressure. The unusual behavior fascinates people and makes these fluids fun to play with.

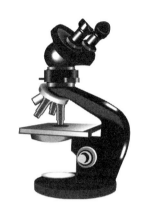

READING:
Mixing Things Up

Some very important scientific discoveries and inventions occurred by accident, or at least unexpectedly. Famous examples include the invention of the microwave oven, stick-on note paper, artificial sweeteners, and **X rays.** Sometimes a scientist struggles for many years before he or she finally makes progress. Thomas Edison (1847–1931) was famous for his hard work and persistence. Did you ever think about how some of your favorite things were invented?

Matter occurs on Earth in three common forms, either as a **gas,** a **liquid,** or a **solid. Molecules** (which are groups of **atoms**) of these forms each behave differently. In a gas, the molecules do not stick together and tend to disperse. Liquids have a specific volume, and the particles stay in contact with each other. Solids are the most rigidly bonded and maintain their shapes.

Isaac Newton (1642–1727) discovered that most fluids flow more easily when they warm up. Fluids that don't follow this rule are called **non-Newtonian fluids.** Their flowing can be affected by pressure. Non-Newtonian fluids are fun to play with because of their surprising behavior.

Many toys are made of interesting materials. Putty-type mixtures in plastic eggs have been popular for years, and other products of chemistry have joined it on the shelves of stores. What chemical mixtures do you know that are made especially for play?

Sir Isaac Newton (Courtesy of The Library of Congress)

A large chemical company's advertising slogan was "Better living through chemistry." What do you think they meant? Can you give examples? When you are mixing materials together to study chemical reactions, think about what you may discover. Chemistry can be messy, experiments use trial and error, and a small change can become a big change. One day you could make a useful compound or mixture. You need to be ready—as famous French scientist Louis Pasteur (1822–1895) said, "Chance favors the prepared mind."

Vocabulary Words

atom .... the smallest unit of an element

gas .... state of matter in which molecules have no definite shape and fill whatever space is available

liquid .... state of matter having definite volume but taking the shape of the container in which it is confined

molecule .... two or more atoms bonded together

non-Newtonian fluid .... fluid whose viscosity (resistance to flow) depends on force applied

solid .... state of matter having definite shape and volume

X rays .... radiation of a specific high-frequency wavelength in which the photons have high penetrating power and can pass through solid objects

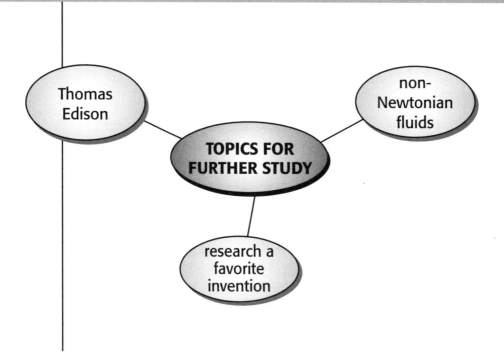

Thomas Edison

non-Newtonian fluids

TOPICS FOR FURTHER STUDY

research a favorite invention

Acids and Bases

Testing Acids and Bases

Acids and bases are substances that neutralize each other. In chemical terms, acids produce positively charged hydrogen atoms or ions (H^+), while bases produce negatively charged molecules of oxygen and hydrogen atoms (OH^-). The measurement scale for the acidity or alkalinity of a substance is called the *pH* (for power of hydrogen) scale.

Both acids and bases have their own set of useful properties, and both can be dangerous. Using gentle, common acids and bases can help students understand some of the identifiable chemical properties associated with each group. Always be careful with chemicals, and avoid contact with skin. Establish good laboratory habits early.

Activity

To test the pH of a liquid, students can dip indicator paper into it and observe the color of the paper. You may choose to purchase indicator paper and have students use the scale that the manufacturer provides, or you can make your own from red cabbage. Chop or shred the cabbage and boil it in distilled water, or water that you know from testing is neutral, until the water turns dark purple. Pour off the water, cool, and soak paper towels in it. Allow the towels to dry and cut them into strips. Students can then dip the strips into liquids and they will change color according to whether the mixture is an acid or a base. Generally, red or pink indicates an acid, while blue indicates a base.

Students can add the water from the cabbage to acids and bases to create a color reaction. The water will change color with acids and bases and is called an *indicator*. Using straws or medicine droppers, have students drip a small amount into some lemon juice to see what happens with an acid. Then they should drip some indicator into a diluted ammonia solution to see a reaction with a base. Try diluting the acid and base solutions with water

Materials per Team

- litmus or pH paper (optional)
- red cabbage
- paper towels
- distilled water or water known to be neutral
- transparent containers for testing liquids
- variety of liquids to test (lemon juice, ammonia, vinegar, dissolved baking soda, fruit juice, soda, etc.)
- scissors
- straws or medicine droppers

and then testing to see if the color changes when the indicator is added. Challenge students to neutralize a solution by combining acids and bases and testing with indicator strips.

What are good solutions to test? Diluted ammonia, vinegar, dissolved baking soda, lemon juice, dissolved corn starch, dissolved aspirin, soap, antacid medicine, or dissolved tablets will yield interesting results. Students can test many common liquids found around home and school. Avoid toxic chemicals and dilute liquids with strong odors, such as ammonia and vinegar.

Rain water or melted snow at different times of year could help students appreciate the dangers of "acid rain." Also, find the pH of soil by mixing it vigorously with water and pouring it through a coffee filter to obtain a testable solution. Various drinks and the cooking water from vegetables will also be interesting. Try the water from a filtered swimming pool to which chlorine is added. (Keep the container capped as chlorine evaporates quickly into the air.)

If students use indicator paper prepared with cabbage juice, have them sort their results by color and try to create a comparative acid/base scale on their own. Remind groups to keep organized lab data.

R E A D I N G:

Learning about pH

Chemistry is the study of the behavior and composition of **matter.** Matter is built up from atoms combining to form **molecules.** Atoms of one **element** (a substance in which all the atoms have the same number of protons) may combine with atoms of other elements to form **compounds.** Water is a common compound, consisting of hydrogen and **oxygen** atoms.

Some compounds can be classified as either acids or bases. Robert Boyle (1627–1691) brought the terms into modern use and used vegetable dyes as indicators (see below). But it took more than two centuries for the chemistry to be explained. Johannes Bronsted (1878–1947) and Thomas Lowry (1874–1936) each independently described the role of ions in **acids** and **bases.**

Ions are atoms or molecules with an **electrical charge.** An acid has a majority of positively charged hydrogen atoms or H^+ ions. A base has more negatively charged **hydroxide** molecules composed of oxygen and hydrogen, or (OH^-) ions. Acids and bases can neutralize each other because H^+ added to OH^- creates H_2O (water).

Both acids and bases have their own set of useful properties, and both can be dangerous. The measure of the strength of an acid or base is called its pH, standing for "power of hydrogen." The **pH scale** ranges from 0 to 14, with 7 representing a neutral value. The farther a substance measures from 7 on the low side, the stronger an acid it is. The higher it measures, the stronger a base it is.

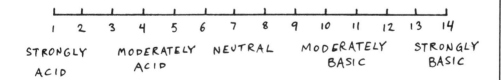

Acids that are weak and safe enough to taste have a sour flavor, while strong acids can burn our skin. Never taste anything in a science lab unless your instructor clearly instructs you to do so. Bases that are weak enough to touch feel soapy or perhaps greasy, but strong bases can burn also. Again, never touch a substance in a chemistry lab unless you are permitted to do so. Luckily, there are safe ways to test for pH without tasting or touching the materials.

Some substances are *indicators*. That means they react and change color with acids and bases. Never rely on taste or touch—use an indicator to test acids and bases. Modern chemical labs even have electronic pH meters.

Vocabulary Words

acid	sour-tasting liquid containing hydrogen ions (H^+)
base	substance that neutralizes acids, removing the hydrogen ions to form water
compound	in chemistry, a substance made up of the atoms of two or more elements bonded into molecules
electrical charge	buildup or capacity of electricity to use force
element	substance composed of one type of atom
hydroxide	chemical compound containing a hydroxyl group, OH (oxygen and hydrogen)
ion	an atom with an electrical charge
matter	anything that occupies space
molecule	two or more atoms bonded together
oxygen	gas that makes up about 21% of Earth's atmosphere
pH scale	scale that indicates whether a solution is acidic or alkaline (base)

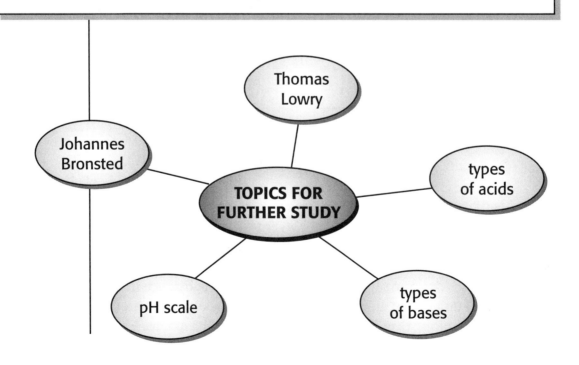

CHAPTER 3

Electricity and Magnetism

TIME LINE

Year	Notable Event
500 B.C.	Thales of Greece experimented with amber.
1100	Compasses were commonly used by Chinese and European sailors.
1269	Petrus Peregrinus wrote a book about magnets.
1600	William Gilbert described Earth as a giant magnet.
1672	Otto von Guericke produced electricity with a mechanical device.
1733	Charles Du Fay discovered the existence of positive and negative electrical charges.
1749	John Canton invented a method for making magnets by rubbing iron pieces together.
1752	Benjamin Franklin built a lightning rod.
1786	Luigi Galvani moved dead frogs' leg muscles with electricity.
1800	Alessandro Volta built a battery.
1820	Hans Christian Oersted announced that electric current produces a magnetic field.
1820	Dominique François Arago learned that electricity passing through a coil produces a magnetic field.
1825	William Sturgeon built an electromagnet.
1827	Andre-Marie Ampere wrote a book about electromagnetic energy.
1831	Michael Faraday invented a transformer and a dynamo.
1855	James Clerk Maxwell explained the theory of electromagnetic waves.
1882	Thomas Edison set up an electrical generating plant.
1897	J. J. Thomson discovered the electron.

Materials per Team

- iron filings (check your science closet— otherwise, these are inexpensive and available at science supply companies)
- oaktag paper
- large locking plastic bags
- overhead and transparency sheets
- variety of magnets

Magnetic Fields

What Does a Magnetic Field Look Like?

In this activity, students will see the shape of a magnetic field.

Activity

A magnetic field is invisible but can be illustrated by mapping its effect on iron filings scattered on a surface. Iron filings are sold by science supply companies and can often be found in old science kits.

When preparing for this activity, keep filings in containers as much as possible when working with younger students. If the filings spill onto magnets, they are hard to remove. More importantly, students can be injured if filings get on their fingers and then they rub their eyes. Transparent plastic bags allow the arrangement of the filings to be seen and projected from the surface of an overhead projector. To project, place the magnet on the projector and place the bag of filings on it. Shake the bag and watch the pattern of the magnetic field emerge.

To begin, have each team of students place a bag of iron filings on a rigid sheet of oaktag suspended across two books. Hold a magnet up to the bottom of the paper and watch the pattern the filings create on top. Have them sketch the magnetic field created by different-shaped magnets, such as a bar, horseshoe, and disk. Does every magnet have two poles from which the magnetic fields emanate?

What other experiments can the students devise? With the oaktag and iron filings set up, modify variables one at a time. To test the strength and size of magnetic fields, vary the distance between the magnet and the filings. Try combinations of magnets and watch the patterns created by the filings.

Leave magnets out on your science tables for the students to explore. Be sure everyone knows not to bring the magnet near electronic equipment. Computer monitors and disks can be ruined by exposure to a magnet.

R E A D I N G:

Discovering Magnetism

Electricity and magnetism are invisible forces that have puzzled people for centuries. The connection between the two wasn't even discovered until the nineteenth century. We now know that an electric current can create a magnet and a magnet can create an electric current. But it took many years of experimenting before these mysterious forces were understood and employed in the service of mankind.

People in ancient times were aware that certain materials in the Earth attracted other materials. A type of rock called **lodestone** was discovered to be a natural magnet attracting iron. **Amber,** a form of fossilized **resin** from pine trees, could be rubbed with a cloth and made to pick up bits of straw. By the 1100s, Chinese and European travelers used **compasses** to help guide sailing ships. But how and why these forces worked remained a mystery.

Petrus Peregrinus (c. 1220– ?) was one of the first scientists to apply the scientific method to the study of magnetism. Peregrinus wrote one of the first science books of the medieval period. Around 1600, Englishman William Gilbert (1544–1603) made a globe from lodestone and demonstrated how a compass reacted to the magnetism of the model Earth. This established the concept of the Earth itself as a large magnet. In 1749, John Canton (1718–1772) invented a method for making magnets by rubbing iron together.

Modern scientists have concluded that the force of a **magnetic field** results from the motion of **electrons.** Electrons are in constant motion but we cannot see them. Scientists living before the twentieth century had a different mental model of an atom and could not describe magnetism as modern physicists do.

Many of the world explorers of the last **millennium** would have been lost without their compasses. Discoveries about the mysterious mechanics of magnetism may have occurred in modern times, but people have used and benefited from magnets for hundreds of years.

Vocabulary Words

amber...fossil form of resin (sticky liquid exuded by plants)

atom ....the smallest unit of an element

compass ....instrument used to determine direction

electrons...................................negatively charged particles in the shell around the nucleus of an atom

lodestone ....magnetized piece of magnetite rock

magnetic field.........................the space around a magnet where its force is in effect

millennium ....a period of a thousand years

resin ....substance produced by plants (and in modern times by human engineers) used to make a variety of products

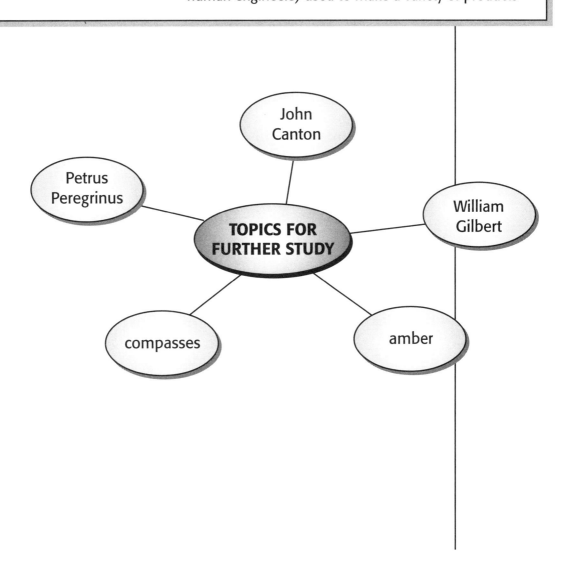

Materials per Team

- C or D batteries
- insulated wire
- directional compass
- oaktag or cardboard
- bar magnet

Currents and Fields

Experimenting with Currents and Fields

Electric current creates magnetic fields. Magnetic fields can create electrical currents. This activity highlights the connection between these complementary invisible forces and lets students demonstrate some of the important discoveries made by scientists such as Christian Oerstedt and Michael Faraday.

Activity

To begin, have students fold a piece of oaktag or cardboard into a U shape to make a holder for the compass. Have them wrap a wire around the cardboard structure, leaving two ends coming out. They should then place a compass inside the oaktag under the wire, lining up the compass needle with the direction of the wire, and connect the ends of the wire to the two ends of the battery. Tell them to note how the compass needle moves. Also, warn them not to hold the wires to the battery for very long at a time as they will heat up and wear down the battery quickly.

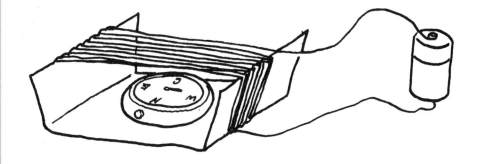

With the battery disconnected, have students turn the compass holder to a new direction and watch the position of the needle. Then they should complete the circuit once again to see the deflection of the compass needle. The magnetic field created by the electrical circuit attracted the compass needle, causing it to turn from its usual bearing of north–south.

Creating an electrical circuit from a magnetic field demonstrates the complementary effect. Make a loop of wire with a diameter that is slightly larger than the width of the bar magnet. Tell them to connect this coil to the ends of the wires leading to the compass holder and push the bar magnet into the coil and then withdraw it. Instruct them to watch the compass needle. They should continue moving the magnet in and out of the looped wire and notice the compass needle move, indicating the presence of an electrical current. Tell them to be sure the coil is far enough from the compass when you do the test. That ensures that the effect is caused by a current in the wire and not by the magnet itself.

R E A D I N G:

Understanding Currents and Fields

In the 1800s, scientists began to unravel the connections between electricity and magnetism. Christian Oersted (1777–1851) brought a **compass** near an **electrical circuit.** The compass needle was deflected at right angles (turned 90° to the current's flow). Reversing the current reversed the compass needle. Oersted had made a great discovery—an electrical current was creating a magnetic field.

Michael Faraday (1791–1867) experimented with the opposite situation. He used a magnetic field to create an electrical circuit. He and Joseph Henry (1797–1878), independently of each other, discovered that electricity can be created, or induced, in a coil of wire by passing a magnetic field through it. Using a compass, Faraday and others could represent and map the force field around a magnet.

We have a mental model of what is going on at the atomic level because of many important advances in understanding. When electricity moves in a circuit, the energy makes **electrons** move along the wire, creating the ability to do work. Electrons are the carriers of the electrical current.

You can find or draw a map of an atom and know which part is the nucleus and where the electrons travel. Some atoms transmit electricity well and are called **conductors.** Others are such poor conductors that they are called **insulators.** They do not allow electricity to pass through them. The copper or other metal part of a wire is a conductor, and the plastic is an insulator.

Measuring electrical current in **voltage** tells how much force is pushing the electrons through the wire. **Amperes,** or amps, tell the rate of flow or current of electrons, how fast the electricity is moving. **Watts** measure how much power the electricity can deliver and how much energy an electrical device is using.

The names of these measurements commemorate great scientists in the field of electricity. Volts are named after Alessandro Volta (1745–1827), who studied ways to store electrical charges. Andre Marie Ampere (1775–1836) discovered relationships between electrical currents. James Watt (1736–1819) built powerful **steam engines** and standardized the measure of force by units called **horsepower.** The electrical unit of force bears his name.

Oersted and Faraday probably did not have as clear a map of **atomic structure** as you do. In science, the best existing theory is considered the one that best fits the data, and every new breakthrough improves the current thinking. Anyone from the nineteenth century would be amazed to see all the work done by electricity in our era. The discoveries of Oersted, Faraday, and scientists of their times have been giant shoulders for many others to stand upon.

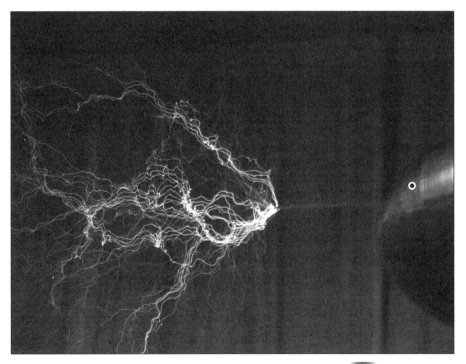

Electrical discharge from a Tesla coil (Photo by Ian Tresman, , courtesy of Wikipedia.org)

Vocabulary Words

amperes.................................... unit of electric current

atomic structure .... how atoms and molecules are built; the form of atoms

compass .... instrument used to determine direction

conductors .... material through which heat and electricity flow easily

electric circuit .... closed path or loop of an electric charge

electrons .... negatively charged particles in the shell around the nucleus of an atom

horsepower .... unit of power equivalent to 746 watts

insulators .... materials that inhibit the flow of heat or electrical current

steam engine .... machine that uses the energy of steam to produce mechanical energy

voltage .... electrical pressure, or the potential difference of an electrical charge

watts .... unit of power

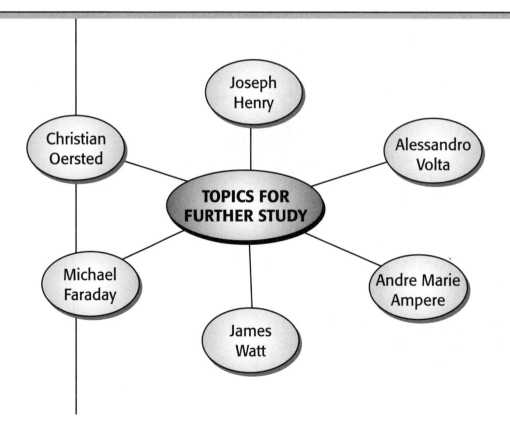

Electromagnets

Making an Electromagnet

This activity demonstrates a connection between electricity and magnetism. Students will send an electric current through a coil of wire and test the resulting magnetic field.

Activity

Have students wind a wire in a tight coil around a pencil. They should then connect the ends of the wire to the poles of a D cell battery. The electric current in the wire creates a magnetic field around the pencil. Tell them to bring the pencil near a pile of paper clips and note how the clips are attracted to it. When the wire is disconnected from the battery and the circuit is broken, the magnetic field disappears and the clips drop.

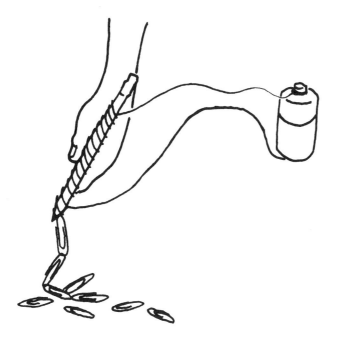

Next, have students use a metal bolt or nail in place of the pencil and see if the magnetic field is stronger. They can wrap masking tape around the bolt several times for insulation. Tell them to repeat the test with the paper clips to compare the field around the bolt to the field created around the pencil.

Have students devise experiments in which they change one variable at a time. Try a different number of loops in the wire coil or a more powerful or weaker battery. After they record the results, discuss them.

If you have iron filings (available from science supply catalogues), spread them on a sheet of paper and bring the electromagnet under the paper. The filings should move into a pattern that displays the magnetic field.

R E A D I N G:

Connecting Electricity and Magnetism

Science often progresses in very uneven steps. It may take many years before something that people experienced long ago can be understood and controlled. Long periods of time may pass before experimentation resumes. Many times an accidental discovery or an individual's inspiration causes a revolutionary change.

The ancient Greeks knew about both magnetism and **static electricity.** By the year A.D. 1100, Chinese navigators used magnetic compasses to guide them. A document about magnets written in **medieval** Europe in 1269 has survived to modern times as the oldest recorded mention of the effect of poles and compasses. Otherwise, not much was written or recorded about electricity or **magnetism** until the **renaissance** of learning in the sixteenth century.

Experimenters in the eighteenth century used a device called a **Leiden jar** to store and discharge static electricity. In 1733, Charles Du Fay (1698–1739) discovered that there are two types of static electricity charges, positive and negative. Charles-Augustine Coulomb (1736–1806) discovered that an inverse square law, similar to the laws of gravity, applied to both electricity and magnetism.

An inverse square relationship exists when, as distance increases, the strength of force decreases by the square of that distance. If you move something twice as far away, the force is four times weaker because four is the square of two. If you move the object three times farther than the original distance, the force becomes nine times weaker, because nine is the square of three.

Recognizing the similarity in the laws and behaviors of electricity and magnetism, Hans Christian Oersted (1777–1851) hunted for a connection between them. Using current electricity, recently developed by Luigi Galvani (1737–1798) and Alessandro Volta (1745–1827), Oersted made a surprising discovery in 1819. Quite by accident, he placed a compass near wires through which electricity flowed. The compass needle was jerked to the side by the current. Oersted published his findings the next year and a flurry of activity and advancement followed.

In 1825, William Sturgeon (1783–1850) created the first electro-magnet. Sturgeon's invention was much like the electromagnets you can make to investigate this interesting **phenomenon**. Andre-Marie Ampere (1775–1836) developed laws and theories explaining how electricity and magnetism affected each other. Shortly after that, in the 1830s, Michael Faraday (1791–1867) and Joseph Henry (1797–1878), working separately across the Atlantic Ocean from each other, found that magnetic fields can generate electricity.

James Clerk Maxwell (1831–1879) explored the mathematics of these electromagnetic fields. He explained that these fields produced waves that moved through space. Although we can't see the electromagnetic waves that are shorter or longer than light waves, they are responsible for the transmission of heat, radio and TV signals, and many other forms of energy.

Understanding how to produce and use electromagnetic energy made possible many of the inventions crucial to the creation of industrialized societies. The **Industrial Revolution** gave rise to the telegraph, light bulb, telephone, electric motor, household current electricity . . . the list stretches on right through to computers and other technologies of the early twenty-first century.

What will the future bring? As you look back on the early 1800s and see the transformation of people's lives by electricity, try to imagine future students looking at the early 2000s and watching today's new technologies move from ideas to products.

Incandescent light bulb (Courtesy of Marco Michelini, stock.xchng)

Vocabulary Words

Industrial Revolution	historical period during which the means of production shifted from home manufacture to machines in factories. The Industrial Revolution is generally considered to have begun in England in the late eighteenth century and lasted well into the 1800s.
Leiden jar	device for building up and storing static electricity
magnetism	having the properties of a magnet
medieval	referring to the Middle Ages, an historical period in European history often considered approximately A.D. 500–1500
phenomenon	an occurrence or fact
renaissance	a revival, a reawakening of cultural achievement
static electricity	accumulation of electrical charge

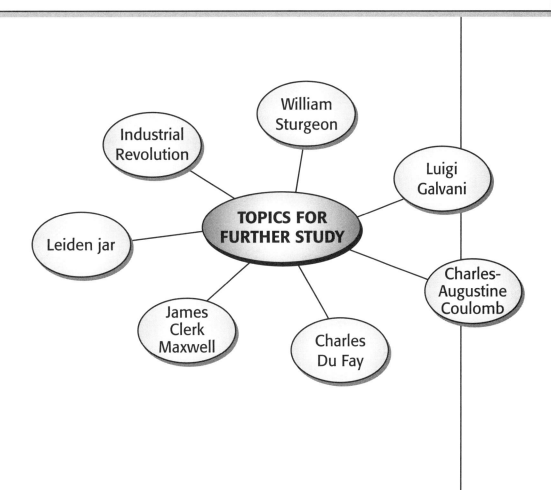

Materials per Team

- pennies and dimes
- insulated wire
- lemon juice
- voltmeter or compass wrapped in wire from "Currents and Fields" activity
- cardboard or thick paper
- scissors
- orange, potato, lemon, and/or other acidic substance
- metal strips (often available from science kits) of copper and aluminum, steel, or zinc
- saltwater solution
- cups
- vinegar, orange juice, lemon, potato, and other test materials

Making a Battery

Building a Battery

In this activity, students will experiment with materials aiming to produce a small electric current. The amount of electricity produced will be small but the activity replicates the work behind the discoveries of Galvani, Volta, and others.

Activity 1

First have students cut the cardboard into small circles and soak it in lemon juice. They can then build a pile of coins and cardboard, alternating dimes and pennies and separating coins with a wet circle of paper. Tell them to be sure the top coin is different from the bottom coin.

To detect whether electricity is produced, use a voltmeter or the wrapped compass from the "Currents and Fields" activity on page 82. Have them hold one lead or end of the insulated wire to the bottom coin and the other lead or wire to the top one. The meter should indicate a small amount of voltage traveling through the circuit.

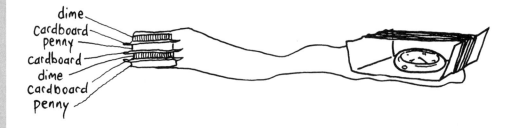

Activity 2

Students can do an additional investigation and make a different sort of battery if you can get metallic strips from a science kit or other source. Have students make a saltwater solution and pour it into three cups. They can then place two strips in each cup and create a circuit similar to the one in the diagram. Again, the meter should indicate the presence of an electrical circuit.

After cleaning the strips, students should attach the strips to the ends of the wire from the meter or compass. Have students place the metal strips into a variety of substances and see if they produce an electrical current. An acidic solution is best, so try using lemon and vinegar, cleaning off the metal strips between tests. Ask: Will sticking the metal strips into a potato create an electrical current?

An electric current is produced by the movement of electrons. The acid solution reacts chemically with the metals, transferring an electrical charge from one to the other across the electrons. The charge continues out along the wire, traveling through the conducting metal that is wrapped inside the insulating plastic. Batteries work in a similar way, using chemical reactions.

AA batteries (Courtesy of Iwan Beijes, stock.xchng)

READING:
Controlling Electricity

In the 1740s, European scientists kept improving a device in which an electrical charge could be built up and then discharged. These came to be called **Leiden jars,** and they could pack a wallop.

Benjamin Franklin (1706–1790) noted the similarity of sparks and sounds that came from Leiden jars to those occurring during thunderstorms. He theorized that **lightning** was a natural discharge of electricity. To prove this, Franklin conducted his most famous experiment in 1752. He connected a Leiden jar to a wire attached to a key flying on a kite in a thunderstorm. While you study the history of science, do not attempt to repeat this dangerous experiment!

Another famous experiment that advanced the understanding of electricity in nature occurred in the 1780s. Luigi Galvani (1737–1798) applied an electrical charge to the muscles of a dead frog's leg. The leg kicked. Galvani had demonstrated how nerve impulses travel in the body.

Although scientists continued to learn more about the nature and power of electricity, they hadn't devised a reliable, steady source to produce a current of electricity.

But soon after Galvani's experiment, Alessandro Volta (1745–1827) created a **battery.** Volta made a "sandwich" using a combination of different metals and a saltwater solution. His battery, like those we use today, produced a flow of electrical charge rather than a burst or static charge like a Leiden jar. The electrons from one of the different metals react with the solution and current flows through the liquid toward the other metal. When a circuit is made, electrons conduct energy around the loop and back through the battery.

Volta's device has changed gradually since 1800. In a typical modern battery, the salt water is replaced by a chemical paste, the battery case is one metal, and a carbon rod held by a brass cap is

Benjamin Franklin

the other. The metal parts of a battery are called **electrodes** and the chemical solution is named the **electrolyte.**

Batteries are generally safe for experiments, but do not take them apart. The chemicals in them can be **caustic.**

Note: *Never experiment with electricity from wall sockets.*

Electricity benefits us by working powerfully but it can be deadly if we accidentally become part of the circuit.

Vocabulary Words

battery	device that produces an electric current through chemical reactions
caustic	likely to burn or corrode substances it contacts
electrodes	a conductor through which electricity passes to enter part of a circuit, or where a charge is stored and emitted
electrolyte	substances that produce ions in water and can carry electrical current
Leiden jar	device for building up and storing static electricity
lightning	natural high-energy electric discharge in the atmosphere

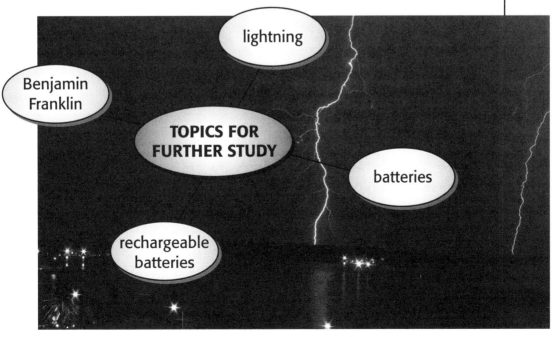

Double lightning (Photo by NikoSilver, courtesy of Wikipedia.org)

Materials per Team

- 1 or 2 C or D cell batteries
- small round disc magnets
- tape
- thin wire (three pieces, 6 to 10 inches long)
- paper clips or aluminum foil
- wire cutter or sandpaper

Motors

Making a Motor

Making an electric motor can be difficult. Many things might frustrate students, so working in groups becomes especially important. Inexpensive motor kits are available from science suppliers and may make this activity easier for some students. If you have younger students, you may need to prefabricate some parts and make a working model ahead of time.

There are several designs of motors from which to choose, and groups can be encouraged to innovate and invent variations. Here's a generic diagram of a basic electric motor model:

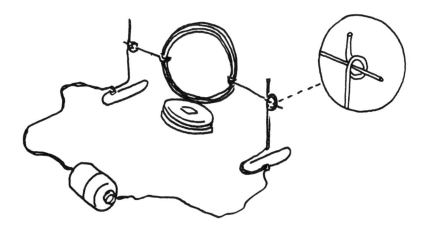

Activity

To begin, have students wrap a thin wire around a battery or a film canister several times. (The number of windings can be a variable to test to extend the activity.) Have them remove the wire and wrap the ends around the loop, maintaining a circular shape. They should try to have the arms directly opposite each other.

Next, they should carefully scrape the insulation off the bottom of the wire's arms. The wire will sit suspended between two paper clip holders bent into loops.

They should then place two or three ring-shaped magnets under the suspended wire loop. They can use tape to attach wires to each end of a battery and connect the other end of each wire to one of the paper clip holders. They might see the loop begin to move. They can give it a spin and see if it continues to turn.

As electric current travels through the coiled wire, an electromagnet is created. Its field overlaps the magnetic field of the permanent magnet. If the poles are alike, they repel, pushing the loop away from the permanent magnet. If the poles are opposite, they attract, pulling the loop down toward the permanent magnet. When the loop turns, the insulated and bare parts of the wire alternate touching the paper clip contacts, causing the push or pull of the magnetic fields to turn off and on. The movement causes the wire loop to spin.

This model differs from commercial motors that have a commutator, a device that alternates current. But the model demonstrates how motion is produced using electric current and the interaction of magnetic fields.

An alternative design uses foil strips as both the path for the circuit and the holder for the loop, eliminating the wires from the battery and the paper clips. Students should place the magnet directly on the battery and fold strips of foil into supports. They can punch holes for the arms of the loop. When students complete the circuit, the loop may spin with a little adjusting.

To extend the activity, allow students to experiment with two batteries versus one, changes in the loop, and other designs for the circuit. Many books of science fair projects and other activity books have simple designs for motors. Encourage interested builders to research and test some prototypes. Build the models ahead of time to determine if your students will be able to complete the activity without undue frustration.

R E A D I N G:
Building Electric Machines

Electric motors do an amazing amount of work in modern society. Look around your home or classroom and you'll probably discover lots of motors. Heating and cooling systems, electronic machines with fans built in, devices with motors to turn discs or cassettes, projectors with lamps that also have fans in them . . . from personal stereos to refrigerators, motors provide many conveniences of modern life.

Electric motors were unheard of before 1820. Electricity itself was not well understood before the nineteenth century, but several key advances happened quickly. Alessandro Volta (1745–1827) developed a battery in 1820. Scientists could use a pile of soaked discs or plates to generate a current of electricity. Also in 1820, Hans Christian Oersted (1777–1851) announced his discovery of the connection between electricity and magnetism.

That same eventful year, Andre Marie Ampere (1775–1836) formulated a law explaining whether electromagnetic fields attracted or repelled each other. Dominique Francoise Arago (1786–1853) also experimented with electromagnetism, learning that a coil of wire can become a magnet. Earlier, people believed iron was necessary to produce a magnet.

Michael Faraday (1791–1867) is considered the inventor of the first electric motor. Faraday was poor while growing up in England. Working in the publishing trade, he read avidly and became interested in science. By attending lectures and working with other scientists in a club, he learned about the rapid advances in electricity. Faraday obtained work with Humphry Davy (1778–1829), a famous British scientist, and Faraday's career took off. He made important discoveries about **elements** by using **electrolysis.** Electrolysis is the process of splitting **compounds** by passing electricity through them. His greatest fame came from his work with electromagnetism.

Faraday reasoned that if electricity could produce a magnetic field, perhaps the reaction could be reversed. His experiments in 1821 showed that motion could be produced when magnets and electric currents interacted. He rotated a magnet around a wire carrying a current. Another part of the wire moved around a stationary magnet. This simple demonstration taught the basic idea for an electric motor.

In 1831 Faraday went on to make a **dynamo,** a device in which an electromagnet is used to produce a current. He also developed the first **transformer,** a device in which the number of turns in a coil of wire can cause an increase or decrease in the current produced by another nearby coil of wire. Together, the motor, transformer, and dynamo became the essential building blocks for the practical use of electricity.

An American scientist, Joseph Henry (1797–1878), worked independently on many of the same projects as Michael Faraday. Henry helped apply the scientific advances to useful inventions, such as the **telegraph** and industrial electromagnets for lifting heavy loads.

James Clerk Maxwell (1831–1879) translated his countryman Faraday's theories of electromagnetism into mathematical language. By the end of the 1800s, most scientists pictured electromagnetism as fields filled with lines of force. In the same way iron filings show a picture of the force field around a magnet, Maxwell extended this model to other forms of energy. Maxwell imagined **light, heat,** and a **spectrum** of other **electromagnetic** forces radiating in waves of different lengths. We can see only a sliver of this spectrum with our eyes—**visible light.** Waves that are longer or shorter than those of light are invisible to us.

Electric fan (Courtesy of Wikipedia.org)

In the twentieth century, scientists continued to push the understanding of **radiation** to create new theories about gravity and the nature of matter and energy. Michael Faraday built outward from his knowledge of magnetic objects and electric currents and investigated the fields around them. He and those who followed changed the course of physics, allowing for new understanding of the forces surrounding us.

Vocabulary Words

compound .... in chemistry, a substance made up of the atoms of two or more elements bonded into molecules

dynamo.................................. device in which an electromagnet produces a current

electrolysis .... chemical change produced by passing electricity through an electrolyte

electromagnetism.................. type of radiation that travels in the form of waves

element................................. substance composed of one type of atom

heat...................................... form of energy resulting from particle motion

light...................................... visible part of the electromagnetic spectrum

radiation .... energy emission by means of waves or particles

spectrum .... sequence or range of energy by wavelength

telegraph .... communication device that sends electrical signals through wires across distances

transformer........................... device that causes an increase or decrease in current

visible light........................... the part of the electromagnetic spectrum perceivable to human eyes

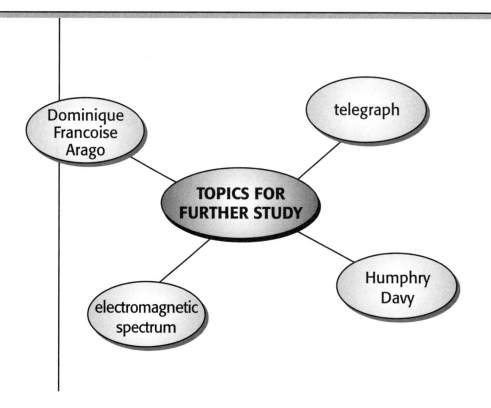

Circuits

Hidden Circuits

Materials per Team

- C or D battery
- insulated wire
- flashlight bulbs
- tape
- cardboard
- metal paper fasteners
- oaktag

Here is a way to practice making electrical circuits while creating a quiz game or study guide. Each team of students can make a question-and-answer board. Answering a question correctly will light up the bulb on this circuit.

Activity

To start the activity, students should punch or poke two parallel rows of holes through the cardboard. They can push a paper fastener through each hole. The first row will represent the questions and should be numbered. The other row, the answers, should be labeled with letters. (See the drawings on page 102.)

Each team should secretly connect each numbered paper fastener to a separate lettered paper fastener with individual pieces of wire on the underside of the cardboard. Be sure they keep track of the combinations and use a random pattern. For example, 1 >>>>D, 2 >>>>A, 3 >>>>F, and so on. Don't let exposed, bare parts of the wires touch anything but the metal fasteners.

Have each team prepare a question-and-answer quiz for the other teams to try. List questions are easiest to set up. For example, numbers could be states or countries, and letters could be capital cities. Think of other matching fact questions—math tables, chemical element symbols, famous scientists and inventors matched to their achievement, and so on.

To make the circuit tester, students should tape one end of separate pieces of wire to each end of a battery. They should wind the free end of one wire around the base of a flashlight bulb, leaving the free end of the other wire unattached.

Students can test answers by placing the free end of the wire on a fastener near a question and the base of the bulb on the corresponding answer. If the bulb lights up, the answer is correct and the circuit is complete. When a team has tested their whole board, have them trade with another team to take a quiz.

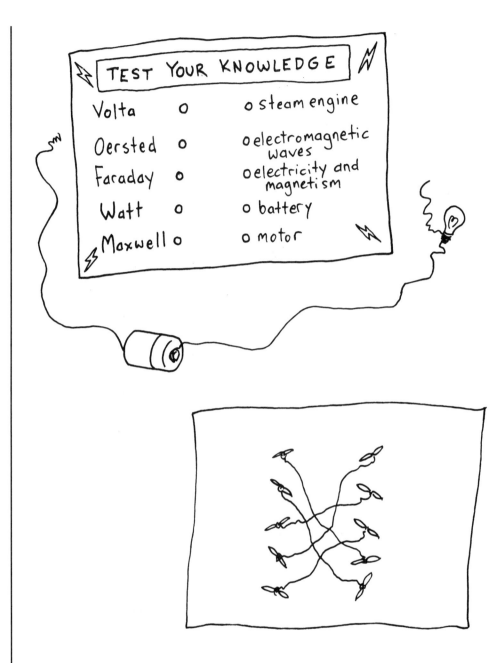

To make the hidden circuit board easily reusable, attach pockets to hold the questions and answers. Fold oaktag into holders (similar to the pockets in library books, only shorter) and tape them into place near the fasteners. Then test makers can place different sets of questions and answers into the pockets. Of course, they'll have to rewire the back once in a while so people don't memorize the circuit arrangement.

READING:
Electricity at Work

Thomas Edison (Courtesy of The Library of Congress)

The great power of electricity was recognized as early as Benjamin Franklin's (1706–1790) famous experiment with his kite in a thunderstorm. Franklin provided a path for electricity to travel down from the sky and into his Leiden jar. Of course, the generator of the charge was a dangerous source and could have ended Franklin's life! What was needed was a reliable, steady source of electricity, and that would take another hundred years to develop.

In order for electricity to power machines and light bulbs and do other forms of work, it has to pass through the device and make a complete circuit. A broken circuit stops the flow of electricity along the path.

Energy moving along a closed path or circuit causes electrons to move and creates an electric current. **Circuit breakers** and **fuses** in electrical panels prevent fires by breaking the pathway to the electrons if there is too much current flowing through the circuit.

When a light bulb burns out, it often means that the **filament,** the small wire bridge inside the bulb that heats up and glows, has broken. Thomas Edison (1847–1931) invented a light bulb that didn't burn out quickly, as others of the time did. The wire contained carbon so it was less likely to burn, and the air had been removed from the bulb.

Edison **patented** many inventions during his career. He developed the system of **three-wire electric supply,** still in use more than one hundred years later. He also designed power stations to distribute electricity to customers.

A **short circuit** occurs when two parts of the pathway connect by accident, creating a shorter path for the energy to travel. Then the electricity bypasses the device it is supposed to power. A short circuit is dangerous because the wires may heat up, causing damage and, possibly, a fire.

When you experiment with electricity using batteries and wires, check the path of energy to the electrons. If it is not a complete loop, your bulb, motor, or other device will not operate. The amount of energy created by one battery may not be dangerous, but a short circuit in a building could be very harmful if the circuit breakers do not respond.

Scientists needed a long time to solve the mysteries of electricity. After a short time, people took it for granted. In the twenty-first century, any interruption of the supply of electricity causes severe disruption.

People are so accustomed to the work done by this invisible form of energy that it is difficult to imagine how recently it was developed. Ben Franklin was once asked what use electricity was. He answered: "What use is a baby?" In Franklin's time, electricity was a baby, and did it ever grow up to be something special!

Vocabulary Words

circuit breaker ....switch that automatically interrupts the flow of electricity when a circuit becomes overloaded

filament.....................................thin wire heated by electricity so that it glows and produces light

fuse ....device designed to protect a circuit by melting when overloaded

patent..the legal statement giving an inventor exclusive rights to make and sell an invention

short circuit..............................when two points in an electrical circuit accidentally meet so the current travels between them instead of on the intended pathway

three-wire electric supply....system used to supply electricity safely to users so that more than one device may be operated at a time

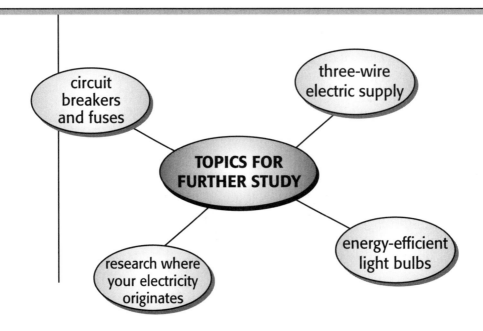

CHAPTER 4
Engineering and Technology

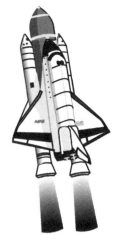

Year	Notable Event
3600 B.C.	Mesopotamians used wheels and carts.
2300 B.C.	Stonehenge built with large stones.
2000 B.C.	Time referred to as the "Bronze Age."
1100 B.C.	Time referred to as the "Iron Age."
250 B.C.	Archimedes built many mechanical devices, including catapults, levers, and water pumps.
200 B.C.	The Chinese used paper, movable type, gunpowder, and other technologies.
1454	The Gutenberg Bible was printed.
1490s	Leonardo da Vinci drew and built many devices, including a parachute.
1608	Hans Lippershey built a telescope.
1668	Isaac Newton built a reflecting telescope.
1673	Anton van Leeuwenhoek reported his findings after using a microscope he built.
1769	James Watt patented his steam engine.
1839	Charles Goodyear discovered the process of rubber vulcanization.
1839	Louis Daguerre produced a photographic image.
1844	Samuel Morse sent his first telegraph message.
1876	Alexander Graham Bell sent his first telephone message.
1877	Thomas Edison built a phonograph.
1879	Edison developed a light bulb.
1888	Heinrich Hertz sent and received radio waves.
1903	Henry Ford began to successfully manufacture automobiles.
1903	Wright Brothers flew an airplane.
1926	Robert Goddard launched a liquid fuel rocket.
1957	Sputnik satellite orbited Earth.
1961	Yuri Gagarin orbited Earth.
1969	Humans explored the moon.

TIME LINE

Materials per Team

- twelve drinking straws
- small paper cup
- twelve paper clips
- scissors
- 1- to 2-inch (3- to 5-centimeter) cubes of modeling clay
- unbreakable objects to use as a weight (each group should have identical objects, such as fishing weights, weights from balance scales, or film canisters filled with sand)
- plates or trays for a building base

Model Skyscrapers

"Necessity Is the Mother of Invention"

Design technology should be a creative and cooperative process. Engineers and other scientists seek the most elegant solutions to problems. Students are also confronted with problems to solve in most areas of the curriculum. As students work on the challenge in this activity, they will practice the general problem-solving technique of generating ideas, evaluating and testing alternatives, and then choosing and refining a strategy. The value gained by working through that process in a team will be at least as important as reaching a solution.

Activity

Each group of students will work cooperatively to solve the same problem, but the outcomes will be quite diverse. Introduce the challenge by stating that a building must be constructed using a specific, limited list of materials. The structure must satisfy two criteria:

1. A weight must be suspended in a cup at least 1 inch (2.5 centimeters) above the base. The building base will be a plate or tray made of paper or plastic.

2. The top of the building must reach 12 inches (30 centimeters) above the base. Think of some of the purposes of tall towers in real structures—communication transmitter, observation tower, or navigational beacon.

Distribute the materials and encourage the teams to discuss and plan before beginning to build. Depending upon the maturity level of the students, you can provide hints and advice, or you can let them approach the task without coaching. For example, here's one way to connect straws using paper clips: Bend open the paper clip and insert the curved ends into the straw openings.

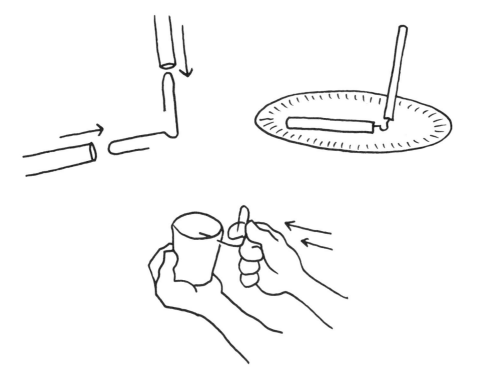

Be prepared to answer specific questions about the design challenge. For example, can the straws be cut to shorter lengths? Decide as questions arise. The rules themselves are not as important as the need for every team to have the same rules.

This activity may be planned with cooperative learning techniques. Students in each team can fill designated roles, such as materials manager, discussion facilitator, recorder, and so on.

When all the groups have constructed and measured their buildings, begin discussion. Teams can compare their solutions to those of the other teams. What is similar about them and what are some important differences? How did the groups stabilize their buildings as the straws reached higher into the air? What other materials would have been helpful?

Encourage understanding of the idea that there are usually multiple solutions to problems. Many inventions and technological improvements have been responses to society's needs. Flip the activity's title around: "Invention is the mother of necessity." Can students think of invented products that have become necessary? For example, many people and organizations couldn't do their jobs without a computer, but perhaps it was the invention of computers that make the job itself necessary. In most cases, inventors create things for which some uses haven't been discovered yet.

READING:
Early Machines

Humans have used machines since before the time of recorded history. For a long time, the use of tools was considered a behavior that separated humans from other animals. Now we know there are some other species that use tools. But so far, no other species comes close to people in the development of tools and technology.

A **machine** is a device that does work, usually by producing and controlling force. You may have learned about **simple machines** in science. Stone axes may have been the first machines. People applied the principles of the **lever** and the **wedge** to get a lot of force working at the end of an axe. Throughout history, humans learned to create more **efficient** machines and continued to gain **mechanical advantage**. Here are simple formulas to explain these terms describing machines:

$$\text{efficiency} = \frac{\text{energy supplied}}{\text{energy put in}}$$

or put another way,

$$\text{efficiency} = \frac{\text{work done}}{\text{energy applied}}$$

$$\text{mechanical advantage} = \frac{\text{force exerted by machine}}{\text{force applied to the machine}}$$

The spread of technology has grown when scientific discoveries are applied and expanded into usable devices. Humans satisfy many needs through machines. Hunting and gathering of food probably spawned many of the early improvements in machines and technology. For example, the harnessing of fire allowed for much greater control over people's environment by providing heat, light, and cooking ability. Technology and science have promoted human capabilities in communication, travel, exploration, shelter, and countless other fields.

Human beings are extraordinary builders. Far back into history, we can find evidence of impressive structures rising in ancient civilizations. You can choose almost any period of history and learn about the tallest and most impressive structures of the time. How were massive materials moved without motors or cranes? When was the first skyscraper built? Some of these questions remain unsolved mysteries.

Stonehenge in England has fascinated people for centuries. Massive pieces of rock rise from a plain as giant arches, all built without benefit of modern machines. The Great Wall of China stretches many miles across rolling terrain. The ancient civilization of Mesopotamia featured towers called **ziggurats** that were to last for many generations, and the Egyptian pyramids stand proudly in Africa to this day. These and many other examples help us to appreciate the long history of human building.

When you build something with a team of fellow student inventors, notice the differences in your project compared to those of other teams. Design challenges usually have multiple solutions.

Some people see a need and work to create solutions. Others like to create new things and then figure out how the invention can be applied. Which attitude do you take—Is necessity the mother of invention, or is invention the mother of necessity?

Stonehenge (Courtesy of Jane Haselden, stock.xchng)

Vocabulary Words

efficient .... description of a high ratio of effort to production

lever .... simple machine consisting of a bar and a fixed point (fulcrum) upon which it may pivot

machine .... a device designed to aid the application of applied force or to help do work

mechanical advantage .... ratio of the output to the input forces. *Mechanical advantage* describes the effect or efficiency of a machine.

simple machine .... simple device that changes the direction or amount of force applied to an object

wedge .... simple machine of one or more inclined planes, used for applying force

ziggurats .... towers built by the ancient Assyrians and Babylonians

Great Wall of China (Courtesy of Alex Seto, stock.xchng)

Lenses

Bending Light

When light travels through a curved surface, it refracts, or changes its course. By focusing the refracted rays of light, we can change our view of the object that is sending us that light. A lens is a curved surface that focuses light rays. In this activity, students will work with lenses and build a model telescope.

Materials per Team

- two magnifying lenses per group
- rulers
- modeling clay
- water
- wax paper
- newspaper
- medicine droppers or straws

Activity 1

To begin, distribute newspaper pages that contain some small print. After students have covered part of their pages with wax paper, have them use the droppers or straws to place single drops of water over different parts of the printing. The water drops will act as lenses and magnify the letters. Encourage students to notice the size of the water drops. Instruct them to examine the size of the drops carefully, and sketch them.

The smaller drops will have a higher degree or power of magnification than larger ones. Discuss possible reasons why.

The smaller drops are steeper. They bend the light at a sharper angle, creating a larger image of the letters. The larger drops are flatter. They cause less of a broadening of the image. Is one better than the other? That depends. Sometimes we need high magnification of a small area (called *field* in optics) and sometimes we need lower magnification that covers a wider field.

Compare the water drops to glass or plastic magnifying lenses. Have them practice moving the lens to focus the image. Younger students should be taught that they should move the lens in between their eyes and the object to be viewed in order to achieve a clear focus. Some lenses will project an inverted image, and students can draw a diagram to trace the path of light through a lens. Some lenses are curved to correct for this inversion. Binoculars, cameras, and some other optical devices use prisms or mirrors to project an image right side up.

Activity 2

Some telescopes, including most early ones, used a combination of lenses to refract the light from distant objects and magnify the image. Galileo made many famous observations about the moon, Venus, and Jupiter with a refractor telescope. Isaac Newton developed telescopes that used mirrors to reflect the image. That type is still called a *Newtonian,* or *reflector telescope.*

To see how a refractor telescope works, have students attach one lens to a ruler with modeling clay. Tell them to look through another lens while they move it along the ruler. They should watch the way it brings distant objects closer. When the view is best, they can attach the second lens with clay and hunt for targets to observe.

Telescope (Courtesy of Nida Rehman, stock.xchng)

READING:

Helping Our Eyes See

When light rays bend, or refract, the images they are carrying can change. Put a spoon in a glass of water and look at it from the side. The spoon can appear to be bent or broken. It might look bigger than it did out of the water. Light traveling between the spoon and your eyes has to pass through water, glass, and air on its way to you. When the rays cross a border between materials, they often change course. Sometimes the change makes it easier to see what the light rays have bounced off.

People have been fascinated by the nature of light as far back as our recorded history goes. Lenses and mirrors were used far back in history for concentrating heat, and eyeglasses have been worn since the 1200s. However, unlocking some of the secrets of how light behaves has proven to be a major challenge.

Isaac Newton (1642–1727) was one of the first scientists to explore light with experimental techniques. He passed light through a **prism** and experimented with the resulting **spectrum,** or rainbow of colors. Since Newton's time, debates occurred over whether light is composed of particles, waves, both, or something else. By the twentieth century, most scientists agreed that light behaves sometimes like waves and sometimes like particles.

Hans Lippershey (1570–1619) is usually credited with the invention of the telescope in 1608. The Dutch eyeglass maker put two lenses together and found that the pair produced a magnified image of distant objects. Galileo (1564–1642) was also a telescope maker. He turned his telescope toward the night sky and advanced the study of astronomy several giant steps, observing the moon and planets. Newton invented a type of telescope that still bears his name. **Newtonian telescopes** use curved mirrors instead of lenses to concentrate the light from distant objects.

Another Dutch craftsman, Anton van Leeuwenhoek (1632–1723), produced a very effective microscope in the 1600s. He observed tiny creatures in drops of water, organisms never seen before. Van Leeuwenhoek's discoveries changed the course of life sciences forever. Because many of nature's secrets are revealed in the details, a microscope opened a new world of miniature wonders to curious observers.

Modern investigators can use an **electron scanning microscope,** an instrument that can project tiny structures at enormously high **magnifications.** Electron microscopes use a beam of **electrons** rather than light rays to reflect off the object being viewed.

As you experiment with simple magnification devices, imagine how exciting it must have been for people to see the surface of the moon or the cells of a leaf for the first time. If you have not explored the world with a microscope or telescope before, you will be in for a treat when you do.

Microscope (Courtesy of David Duncan, stock.xchng)

Vocabulary Words

electron scanning microscope	device in which a beam of electrons contacts a specimen and creates a highly magnified image of it
electrons	negatively charged particles in the shell around the nucleus of an atom
magnification	to increase the size or image of an object
Newtonian telescope	telescope that magnifies an image by reflecting light off mirrors
prism	triangular clear material (like glass) that separates white light into its colors
spectrum	sequence or range of energy by wavelength

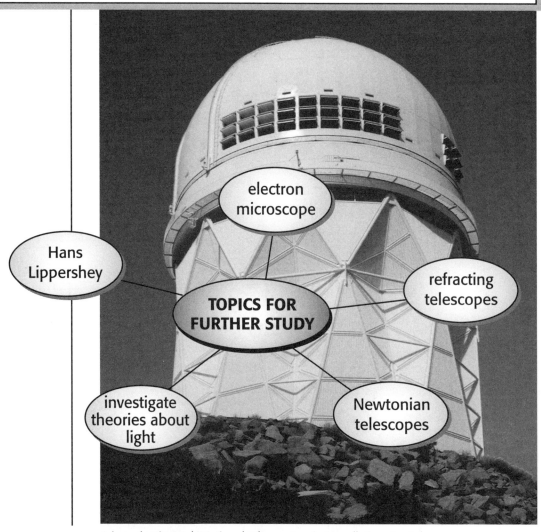

Arizona's Kitt Peak National Observatory's Mayall 4-meter telescope
(Courtesy of NOAO/AURA/NSF)

Phonographs

Groovy Sound

The ability to record and play back music and other sounds created a major change in home entertainment. Records provided people with a way to hear performances whenever they chose. Technology inevitably changes and records have been replaced by other media. There are still many records around, however, and if you can find the materials, this activity provides learning in several areas. Students can experiment with producing sound as well as having experience with a historical technology.

Activity

Have students roll up and tape sheets of paper into cone shapes. When students hold these "megaphones" up to their ears, have them notice the differences in hearing sounds. Ask: Are softer sounds amplified? Do they hear more from one direction?

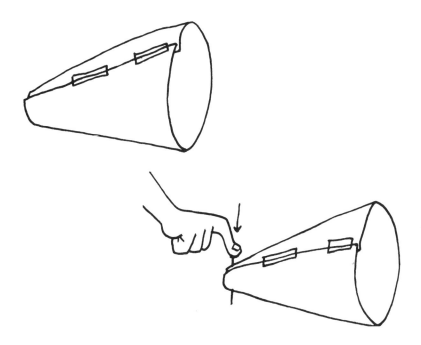

Materials per Team

- phonograph records (not valuable ones, as they can get scratched)
- straight pins
- paper and tape
- turntables, or pencils to use as spindles for rotating records
- magnifying lenses (optional)

117

Next, have students carefully examine phonograph records, using magnifying lenses if available. Tell them to note the grooves that spiral around the disk from the outer edge toward the center. Discuss how a phonograph works: a needle, or stylus, travels through the grooved path while the recorded disc rotates on a turntable.

Students should prepare their playback devices by carefully pushing a pin through the narrow end of the cone. Have them rotate the records by spinning them on a pencil if no turntables are available. (Check old school closets for discarded record players and save them. A mechanical turntable has lots of uses!) Otherwise, turn on the record players and have the students take turns holding their cones lightly over the records and letting the pins track gently through the grooves. With practice and a soft touch, music from old "platters" will be heard in the room as if by magic.

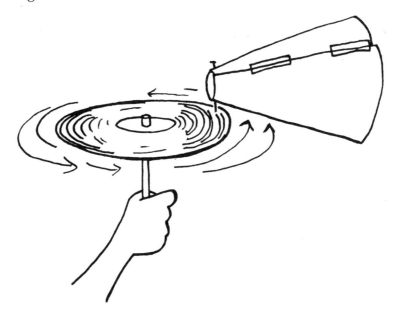

Even old record players used electricity to amplify sound, sending signals through wires and causing speakers to vibrate. But this activity demonstrates the underlying principles of a needle producing sound by following a grooved path. The grooves cause the needle to vibrate and the recorded sound is played back.

Warning: *This activity will scratch and degrade the records. Do not use any records that are considered collectible items. Never use anyone's records for this activity without permission.*

READING:
Recording Sounds

Among the many inventions of Thomas Edison (1847–1931), the **phonograph** ranks as one of the most popular and influential. The process brought recorded performances to millions of people at any time they chose.

Sound travels by **waves** produced by vibrations. Edison and others discovered that these vibrations could be focused on a stretched material, or diaphragm. The diaphragm would vibrate and cause a needle to carve lines or grooves in a turning cylinder covered with tin foil. When the process was reversed and the needle traveled along the grooves, the vibrations played back the original sound. In 1877, Edison recorded and played back the nursery rhyme "Mary Had a Little Lamb."

Eventually the technology changed. Flat disks replaced cylinders and durable plastic replaced tin foil and wax. Emile Berliner (1851–1929) was one of the first inventors to use disk "records" in 1904. The recorded music industry boomed in the twentieth century.

Using electricity allows sound to be transmitted (sent) and amplified (made larger or louder). As the needle rides through the grooves on a record and vibrates, it moves a magnet attached to it. The magnet is positioned between wire coils and causes an electrical signal to be generated. A device called an **amplifier** can boost the signal enough so that it can cause a **loudspeaker** to vibrate and project the sound.

Simply running a needle through the grooves of a record produces sound. The sound can be amplified through a cone-shaped paper, or megaphone. Using a steady hand or motor-driven turntable allows us to hear the record pretty clearly.

What machines are used now to reproduce recorded sound? **Compact discs,** or CDs, replaced magnetic tapes and records in the late twentieth century. They work very differently.

Digitally recorded sound is stored as a series of bits of information. Instead of a bumpy path for a needle to follow, a CD has tracks of data stored as tiny pits. The pits are read by a **laser** that transmits the information to a processor. So don't run a needle over a CD and expect to hear music!

Vocabulary Words

amplifier .... device that increases a signal

compact disc (CD)................. device used for storing data in a digital format.
A laser beam reads the sequence of pits in the disc.

laser .... acronym for "**l**ight **a**mplification by **s**timulated
emission of **r**adiation," a device that produces a
concentrated beam of light

loudspeaker............................. device that converts electrical signals into sound

phonograph............................. machine used to play back sound recorded on
records, hard plastic discs with grooves. As a record
turns, a needle travels through the grooves, vibrating
and reproducing the recorded sound.

waves... energy that travels across space as motion or
disturbance

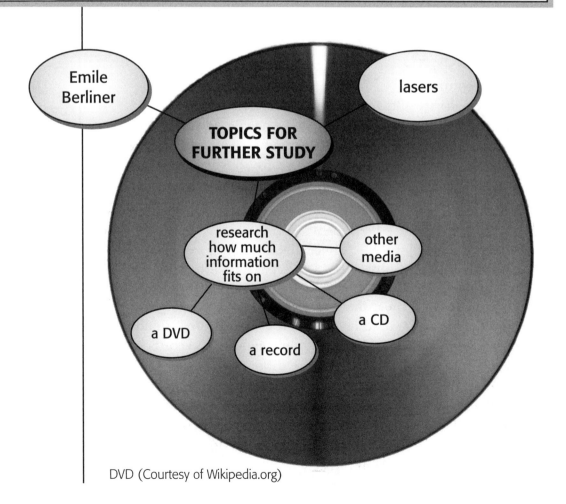

DVD (Courtesy of Wikipedia.org)

Animation

Motion Pictures

The human eye will retain an image for a fraction of a second after the image is removed. That's why we can look at a series of pictures and see a coherent, smooth record of action. Movies are projected when a light is shone through a series of pictures being moved quickly in front of a lens. Our eyes help our brain smooth out the show by ignoring the brief periods between the pictures. We combine the photos or drawings into a continuous lifelike flow.

Students can work with this optical property to create cartoons and gain an understanding of how motion pictures work. Following are three suggested activities.

Materials per Team

- drinking straws
- index cards
- sturdy paper
- scissors
- mirror
- large round plastic bottle or jug
- blank paper

Activity 1

For the first activity, give each student two blank index cards. Instruct them to draw pictures on both cards. The pictures should be related to each other because the object is for them to trick their eyes into seeing the drawings together. Suggest that they keep the drawings simple and brainstorm some ideas. Examples can include a bird on one card and a tree branch on the other, a dog and a doghouse, and the sun and clouds matched with flowers. Then tell them to staple or tape the cards back-to-back around a pencil. When students roll their pencils rapidly between their hands so that the cards spin, their eyes should see the two drawings simultaneously. After they see how it works, they'll want to perfect their techniques and create new drawings.

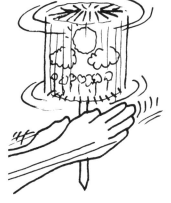

Activity 2

In the next activity, students make picture wheels, or phenakisto-scopes. Each person will cut a disk out of a sturdy type of paper, such as oaktag. Imagining the face of the disk as a clock, they should mark and cut narrow slits at each hour position. Then they draw pictures between the slits showing a sequence of action. Once again, brainstorm suggestions to help vary the cartoons: a person jumping, a bird flapping its wings, a box opening, and so on.

Have students stick a toothpick through the center, or pin the disk to a pencil eraser. They should aim the picture side of the disk toward a mirror and spin the disk close to their eyes while looking through the slits. They can watch the cartoon in the mirror.

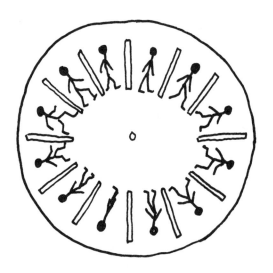

Activity 3

A zoetrope uses the same principles to create motion pictures. The pictures can be changed more easily and the image is not viewed in a mirror. Each group will need a large plastic container. Use either a jug or bottle that's been cleaned or a tub-type container. The container will need slits cut out to look through. Students can draw pictures on strips of paper cut to fit around the inside of the container. When they spin the zoetrope, what they see as they look through the slits will make the sequence of pictures seem like an animated cartoon.

Have students figure out ways to spin their zoetropes. Sticking a pin through the bottom of the container into an eraser as a base may work best for a short, wide container. As an alternative, they can leave the top on a jug-type container and attach a string to it for hanging. Devising ways to operate their machines will sharpen their inventing skills.

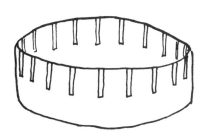

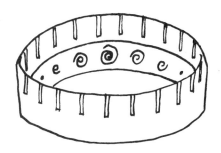

Modern replica of a Victorian zoetrope (Photo by Andrew Dunn, courtesy of Wikipedia.org)

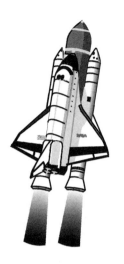

READING:
Telling Stories with Pictures

Almost everyone enjoys going to the movies. The big, bright screen in the large, dark room shows images so real that we can get lost in the story. Compared to other forms of storytelling, motion pictures are very young. It was only in the early twentieth century when motion pictures began to change from a novelty to a major form of entertainment, and sound wasn't a part of the show until 1926.

Thousands of years before the technology was produced, people knew about the physical sensation that makes movies possible. It's called *persistence of vision*. The Roman poet Lucretius (c. 95 B.C.–55 B.C.) wrote about it in the first century B.C. Here's how it works:

When light enters our eyes and strikes the **retina,** light-sensitive nerve cells send an electrical signal to the brain. The eye retains the image for a fraction of a second. The brain fills in the spaces between images by holding on to a view of what we've seen. So we see movement as a smooth, continuous process rather than as a jerky set of still images.

A motion picture is a series of still images projected rapidly in a sequence. Before there were machines and light bulbs, people drew pictures to make the moving images. In 1825, Dr. William Fitton (1780–1861) invented a toy called the **thaumatrope** in England. The viewer spun a disk or card with different pictures on each side, giving the illusion of one image. The most familiar image shows a bird on one side and a cage on the other. When the card moves quickly, the pictures merge and the bird seems to be in the cage.

More elaborate devices soon followed. In 1832 Joseph Plateau (1801–1883) of Belguim invented the **phenakistoscope.** That device had two circular disks, one with slits in front of one with drawings. When the disks spun and a person looked through the slits at the pictures, persistence of vision created an object in motion.

Beginning in the 1860s, people began to enjoy a toy called a **zoetrope.** William Horner (1786–1837) invented the first zoetrope in 1834. A strip of pictures is placed inside a rotating wheel. The effect is striking when the drawn object appears to move. But the action is very limited. Early motion pictures couldn't tell much of a story with just a few frames of pictures.

The invention of photography led to the development of longer and more realistic movies, but the technology to make photographs into movies took almost one hundred years. In 1822, Joseph Niepce (1765–1833) of France produced a **positive image.** About 1839, his countryman, Louis Daguerre (1787–1851), developed a reliable process for printing **daguerrotypes** on copper plates. By 1848 an English inventor named Frederick Archer (1813–1857) described capturing an image on a **negative plate** and printing it.

Of course, because copper plates are heavy and block light, they cannot be run past a lamp at many frames per second. A lighter, translucent material was needed before images on film could be projected. The invention of roll film by W. H. Walker in 1884, and George Eastman's (1854–1932) machines to produce it in 1885, created a way to make many pictures on a small, flexible material. The technology of photography took off rapidly, and Etienne-Jules Marey (1830–1904) built a camera that could take many pictures quickly.

Louis Daguerre (Courtesy of Wikipedia.org)

Thomas Edison (1847–1931) and others developed machines that would run a loop or roll of film around endlessly and could be viewed through a "peephole." Light beneath the film illuminated the image. Only one person could watch the film at a time, limiting the audience severely. In the 1890s, inventors in Europe and the United States built projectors, and movies began to be shown in large halls. The entertainment industry was born.

The history of motion pictures in the twentieth century started with silent movies being curiosities and grew to be a huge part of people's lives. Hollywood became a center for American culture. Television, popularized in the 1950s, was expected by some people to cause the end of the movie business. But the VCR, or **video cassette recorder,** allowed people to watch movies at home on their TVs. The next innovations were the **digital video disc,** or DVD, player, and the digital video recorder, or DVR. The motion picture industry has survived all these changes and flourished. What do you think the future of entertainment will be?

Vocabulary Words

daguerrotypes .... photographs made on copper plates

digital video disc (DVD) ..... device that records and stores data that can be shown visually

negative plate .... in photography, a piece of film on which an image formed after a chemical reaction. Dark areas of the object depicted appear light and light areas appear dark. When a photograph is printed, the areas of the image become a positive, or actual likeness.

phenakistoscope .... device in which a spinning disk is observed through another disk with slits cut out. The observer has the illusion of seeing a motion picture.

positive image .... in photography, the image or actual likeness. Compare to *negative*, which carries the opposite image so that dark areas represent light sections and vice versa.

retina .... light-sensitive layer of cells in the eye

Vocabulary Words *(continued)*

thaumatrope .... toy that simulates motion by quickly alternating pictures from one side of a card to the other

video cassette
recorder (VCR) .... device that records and plays video programming using magnetic tape contained within a cartridge or cassette

zoetrope .... a rotating wheel of drawings that simulates a motion picture

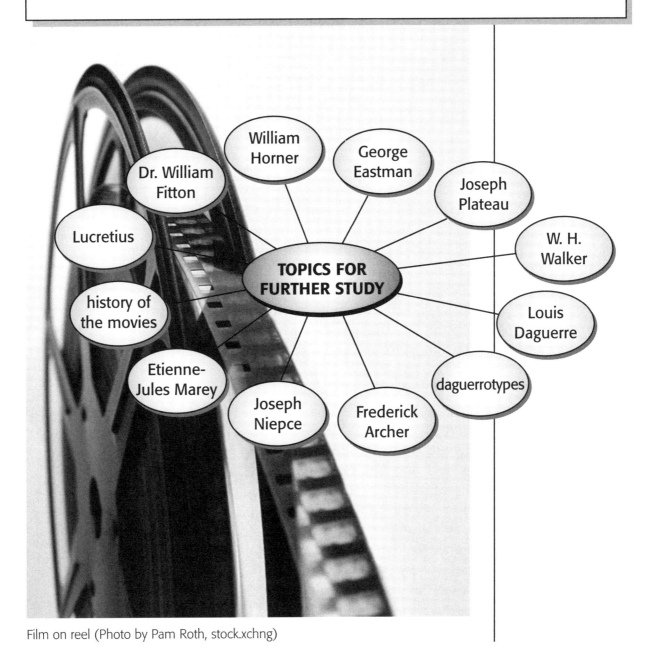

William Horner

George Eastman

Dr. William Fitton

Joseph Plateau

Lucretius

W. H. Walker

history of the movies

TOPICS FOR FURTHER STUDY

Louis Daguerre

Etienne-Jules Marey

Joseph Niepce

Frederick Archer

daguerrotypes

Film on reel (Photo by Pam Roth, stock.xchng)

Materials per Team

- batteries
- switch (optional)
- safety goggles
- hammers
- wire
- nails
- block of wood
- thin strip of metal

The Telegraph

Dots and Dashes

Telegraphs could send electrical signals along wires to distant locations. Electromagnetic technology allowed a sender to tap in a two-character alphabet (short and long, or dots and dashes), which was heard by the receiver. The telegraph provided the first long distance "real time" communication system. This activity will demonstrate how electromagnets can be applied to a specific problem. In this case, the problem is how to send a message a long distance in a short time.

Activity

Before beginning, be sure students have had some experience with electromagnets or at least understand that a current flowing in a coil around a metallic object creates a magnetic field. Then have students connect one end of a wire to one end, or terminal, of a battery. They should connect the other end of the wire to a switch or leave it free to touch the other wire when it is time to close the circuit. They will need a second wire to conduct electricity from the other terminal of the battery, through the telegraph "receiver," and back to the first wire or a switch.

To make the receiver, make sure students have put on their safety goggles. Then have them drive two nails into a block of wood. The nails need to be fairly close together. They should bend a thin piece of metal so that it sits just above the two nails; they may need to make it into a z shape. They should then attach the metal piece to the block of wood with another nail. Have

them wrap the second piece of wire around one nail and then the other and bring the end of the wire back to the switch, or near the loose end of the first wire. When they close the switch or touch the wires together, the nails become electromagnets and pull the metal down. When they break the circuit, the metal springs back up.

Students can look up Morse Code on the Internet and then practice, or they can make up a code for themselves. How far apart can they place the sender and receiver and still send messages?

Computers use binary code, turning switches on and off to send information in small bits. The telegraph revolutionized communication in its day as the computer has in more modern times. But if students list similarities and differences between the telegraph and their own instant messaging technology, they'll appreciate the continuum that has produced today's tools.

Samuel Morse's electric telegraph (Courtesy of Wikipedia.org)

READING:

Sending Messages across Wires

Think of all the ways there are to send a message. Telephone conversations, answering machines, electronic mail (e-mail), and U.S. Postal Service letters, to name a few. When and how do you think all these methods were developed?

The history of people communicating across distances probably goes back before written language was common. Drums could send sound **waves** through miles of air, and smoke rising from signal fires surely attracted lots of attention. People first carried messages and stories in their memories, then later in written forms, as they traveled. When humans learned to use electricity, communication changed forever.

One important invention that changed history is not heard from much anymore—the telegraph. But many of the changes the telegraph brought paved the way for its modern **high-tech** descendants. Samuel Morse (1791–1872) invented the telegraph. He used the principles of **electromagnetism** to send messages through wires. When a telegraph operator pressed a key on a **transmitter,** electricity would travel to another telegraph's receiver that might be far away. The electrical current would create an electromagnet in the receiver and tap a metal bar. Long and short taps would be sent and received. Words would be read from those "dots and dashes" tapped out by the telegraph according to an alphabet known as Morse Code. Samuel Morse not only invented the telegraph but also a code to use with it.

As the United States grew to stretch from ocean to ocean, telegraph wires kept regions in touch with each other. But in the 1870s, the telephone was born, and soon actual sounds were traveling through wires. By the later years of the twentieth century, **wireless communication** became common and people almost everywhere could send and receive messages instantly.

Vocabulary Words

electromagnetism..................type of radiation that travels in the form of waves

high-tech ....nickname for specially designed, advanced devices

transmitter ....device that converts sound or other form of information into electrical signals and radiates it to receivers

waves..energy that travels across space as motion or disturbance

wireless communication .....general term for sending signals without wires connecting the transmitter and receiver

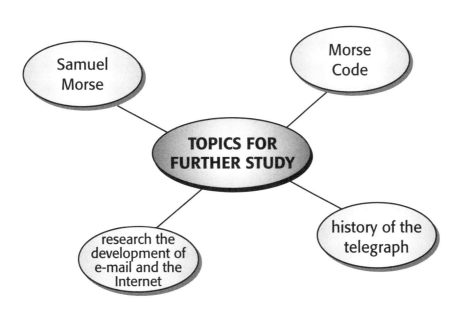

Materials per Team

- balloons
- paper
- plastic bags
- string or dental floss
- drinking straws
- inflating pump (optional)

Rocketry

Blast Off!

In the twentieth century, rocket ships changed from science fiction to real science. Students can use their creativity while applying some principles of physics to make and test balloon rockets. Provide the same materials to each team of builders and see how the designs vary.

Activity

Rockets work primarily by two principles known as Newton's first and third laws of motion. The first law states that objects in motion tend to stay in motion, and objects at rest stay at rest, unless an external force acts upon them. The third law states that every force or action has an opposite and equal reaction. Inflating a balloon and then releasing it can illustrate these laws. As an introduction to this activity, have students inflate balloons, squeeze the neck between their fingers, and then let go.

A balloon will stay on Earth because of gravity and remain earthbound until another force acts upon it. Releasing the air and allowing it to rush out the neck of the balloon creates an opposite reaction—the balloon is thrust through the air. When all the air escapes, gravity pulls the balloon back to Earth. In space, beyond the pull of gravity, the balloon would continue until another force stopped it.

Students can work in teams to make a variety of balloon rockets. First, have them make a cone of paper. They can tape the paper and place it over the balloon. Tell them to let the air escape and see how high the cone flies.

For a more controlled rocket, have them tape a straw to a bag and run a string or dental floss through the straw. They can then place the balloon in the bag, inflate it, and release the air to propel the bag along the string. they will be challenged to refine the design of these rocket-powered monorails (see the illustration on page 133).

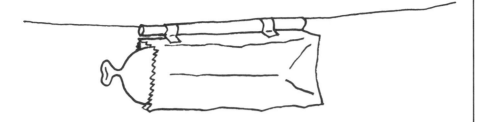

Be sure students do not place their lips on balloons where others have inflated them already. Blowing up balloons may be difficult or impossible for some students. Plastic pumps with blunt nozzles designed for balloons are available at toy stores. Otherwise, be sure that someone on each team can do the inflating.

CRISTA-SPAS-2 in orbit on August 7, 1997 (Courtesy of NASA)

READING:

Exploring Space

The "space race" began in the 1950s, when rockets were first sent up fast enough and far enough to avoid falling back down. "What goes up must come down" was no longer true! In fact, the second satellite ever launched into orbit by the United States was Vanguard 1, which blasted off on March 17, 1958. As the end of the twentieth century approached, Vanguard 1 was still in orbit.

The steps to space flight began long ago. Isaac Newton's (1642–1727) laws of motion and his explanation of gravity are part of every rocket scientist's background. But even before Newton's time, people had learned how to propel rockets through the air. In China, rockets were used as early as the middle of the twelfth century. In the fourteenth century Italian city-states used rockets as weapons.

In Russia, where the first satellite would be launched, rocket science began to flourish in the late nineteenth century. Konstantin Tsiolkovsky (1857–1935) calculated the speed necessary for an object to break free of Earth's gravity, a figure later named *escape velocity*. To reach orbit, an object must travel about 8 kilometers per second (km/sec.; about 5 miles/second). To leave Earth's pull completely, a speed of 11.2 km/sec (40,250 kilometers per hour or about 25,000 miles per hour) is necessary. Another Russian, N. I. Kibalchich (1850–1881), actually built a rocket in 1881. Unfortunately, he also built bombs, one of which killed Czar Alexander II, the ruler of Russia, and Kibalchich was executed.

Robert Goddard (1882–1945) is regarded as one of the most important pioneers in rocketry. Goddard built and launched a liquid fuel rocket in 1926 that reached a height of 56 meters (184 feet) and traveled at 97 km/hr (60 mph). Three years later, he launched the first rocket to carry instruments, sending a thermometer, barometer, and camera aloft.

War prompted more advances in rocket technology. German engineers, including Wernher von Braun (1912–1977) and Willy Ley (1906–1969), built V-2 rockets capable of traveling 1 mile per second (mi/sec). These rockets were used against England in World War II. After the war, Von Braun and Ley used their skills

in the United States space program. In 1949, a two-stage rocket using the V-2 blasted upward to 400 kilometers. In 1958, the first American satellite was carried into orbit by a rocket named Jupiter.

The 1950s and 60s were the time of the Cold War, an uneasy period of international tension between **superpowers.** The Soviet Union and the United States were locked in competition to develop more powerful and strategically important weapons. They engaged in a space race as well as an arms race. In 1957, the Russians launched Sputnik 1, the first artificial satellite to orbit the Earth. (The moon might be considered a natural satellite of the Earth.) The United States countered by devoting more money, time, and education to its space program. Both nations were eager to have their citizens be the first explorers in space.

Accomplishments and milestones happened rapidly. Sputnik 2 followed soon after Sputnik 1 and carried a dog as a passenger. In 1961, Yuri Gagarin (1934–1968) became the first human being in space, orbiting the Earth in 108 minutes. The first travelers to go completely around the world, survivors of Ferdinand Magellan's (1480–1521) crew, had taken 1,084 days to circumnavigate the globe in the sixteenth century!

Space travel technology boomed in the 1960s. "Firsts" became more and more frequent. Alan Shepherd (1923–1998) was the first American astronaut to enter space. Cosmonaut (the Russian name for space traveler) Valentina Tereshkova (1937–) was the first woman to fly in space. The Russians hit the moon with an unmanned spacecraft in 1959, and Americans Neil Armstrong (1930–) and Buzz Aldrin (1930–) stepped upon its surface in 1969.

In the later years of the twentieth century, cooperation began to replace competition in space exploration. **Space stations** were built that housed scientists from several nations, and **shuttle spacecraft** regularly carried international crews back and forth into space. In the quest to establish permanent space stations and to send humans to explore Mars, scientists from different parts of the world are combining their talents.

Throughout the history of human exploration, the world has seemed to become smaller. The time spent traveling long distances has steadily shrunk, and communication links make those distances seem less remote. What will happen in space? A frontier once considered limitless is also getting more crowded. In 1998, there were nearly 10,000 objects large enough to be tracked in Earth orbit. Some are satellites working to transmit and collect data.

However, some of the objects are **defunct** satellites no longer able to do the job for which they were designed. Some orbiting objects have become **space junk,** broken or discarded pieces of equipment held in a path by the Earth's gravity. Remember, not everything that goes up must come down, and once it's up in orbit, it could be there for a while!

What do you think is in store for the pioneers of space travel in the twenty-first century? When will humans reach Mars and other destinations? Having learned to escape the pull of their home planet, the sky is no longer the limit for humans.

Vocabulary Words

defunct	no longer used
shuttle spacecraft	vehicles designed to enter space and return so they can be flown multiple times
space junk	orbiting remnants of man-made objects in space
space station	a long-term manned satellite designed for scientific research
superpowers	very powerful nations that are dominant in world affairs

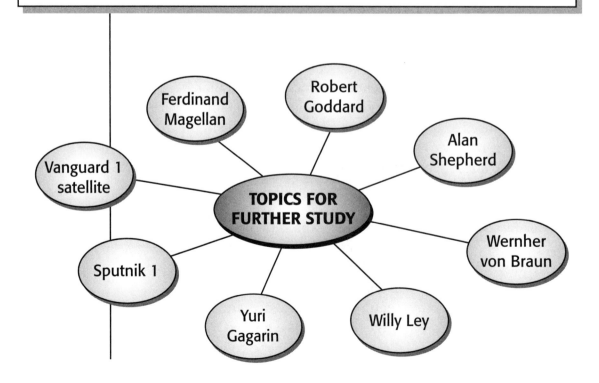

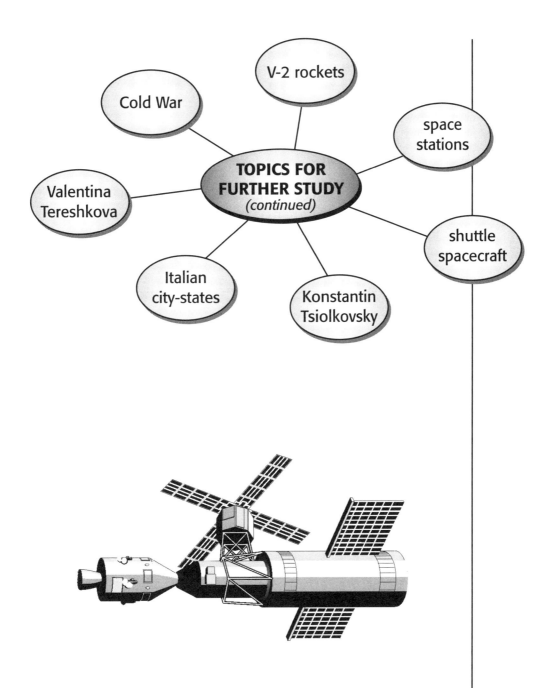

TOPICS FOR FURTHER STUDY *(continued)*

V-2 rockets

Cold War

space stations

Valentina Tereshkova

shuttle spacecraft

Italian city-states

Konstantin Tsiolkovsky

Materials per Team

- white glue
- Epsom salts
- distilled water
- borax soap
- spoons (or other tools for measuring and stirring)
- paper towels
- small cups
- small plastic food storage bags
- wax paper

Bouncing Balls

Bouncing Around

In this activity students will make interesting mixtures. In addition to having fun playing with the mixtures, they'll practice measurement skills while engaging in chemistry activities using safe, common materials.

Activity

Students can make a ball by mixing simple ingredients. Because 1 tablespoon equals 3 teaspoons, the formula is easy to convert into metric units or enlarge proportionally to make bigger bouncers. The "units" measurements in the recipe allow you to work with proportions.

Have students place 1 tablespoon (6 units) of white glue in a small cup. In another cup, have them combine $1/2$ teaspoon (1 unit) of Epsom salts and $1/2$ teaspoon (1 unit) of water and mix to create a solution. They should pour the salt water into the glue and stir. Then they can fold into a paper towel and squeeze out the moisture.

They can roll the mixture into a ball on wax paper. Test it!

Students can experiment with the ingredient ratio in a similar way to the "The Search for the Perfect Mess" activity on page 69. What are the effects of adding more glue, or more salt, or more water?

There are many interesting recipes for putties, slimes, and other entertaining mixtures. As long as materials are not disposed of down the drain, students can create mixtures using glue, water, salt, laundry starch, and borax-based detergents.

Here are other recipes to try:

Remember: *Do not dispose of these mixtures in the drain.*

Putty

- 45 milliliters liquid laundry starch + a pinch of salt

Stir to dissolve. Add 25 milliliters of white glue, and stir 30 strokes. Squeeze out starch and knead. Add more salt as needed.

Modeling Dough

- 3 cups flour
- 1.5 cups salt

Mix and add 1 cup water.

Mix well. Use immediately or store in sealed container.

Slimy Ooze

In a bowl, combine:

- 4 oz. (120 mL) white glue
- 4 oz. (120 mL) distilled water
- Food color (optional)

Mix together to make a watery glue mixture.

In a separate bowl, combine:

- 1 teaspoon (5 mL) borax soap
- 1 cup (250 mL) distilled water

Stir to dissolve as much borax as possible.

Combine both mixtures in a plastic bag and knead.

If it sticks too much, add borax. If it's too gooey, add watery glue.

READING:
Discovering by Accident

Stories about inventions and inventors are often amusing and surprising. Many times a mistake turned out to reveal the key to an important new product or process. Thomas Edison (1847–1931) is quoted as saying "Genius is 90% perspiration and 10% inspiration." Throw in a dash of chance and luck and you'll have a recipe for inventing. Here are some examples of interesting inventions, and some suggestions for further exploration.

Rubber is a natural substance produced by rubber trees. Rubber has many wonderful properties, but raw rubber is only workable in a narrow temperature range. When it's too cold, rubber cracks. When it's too hot, it melts. In the 1830s, scientists were trying to find out how to avoid these breakdowns. They added different chemicals to rubber to try to change it.

Charles Goodyear (1800–1860) worked on the rubber problem. He had no success until one day in 1839 when he accidentally dropped a mixture of rubber and sulfur onto his stove. The awful smell prompted him to clean up the mess quickly. To his surprise, he found the rubber soft but not melted. Goodyear had discovered a way to process rubber to a useful state. He named the procedure **vulcanization.** Tires, raincoats, sneakers, and thousands of other products followed.

In 1903, Eduoard Benedictus (1878–1930) was experimenting with a liquid substance called **cellulose nitrate** when he dropped a glass flask. The flask broke but did not shatter into small pieces. Benedictus realized that the cellulose had kept the glass intact by preventing the broken pieces from separating. He refined the process and soon people could use **shatterproof glass** in windows, eyeglasses, and other places where the risk of injury was high if glass smashed.

An eleven-year-old boy left a stirring stick in a container of juice and forgot about it. When the temperature dropped overnight, Frank Epperson (1894–1983) had accidentally invented a frozen treat. Years later he made up the name *Eppersicle* for it. You probably know the name it made famous when it began to be sold with two sticks.*

*These are now known as Popsicles.

George de Mestral (1907–1990) was pulling burdock seeds off his clothes after being outside when inspiration struck. He developed a fastening system for clothes using tiny hooks and loops in 1948, which he later named *Velcro.*

Maybe you have used a microwave oven. Did you know it was invented by accident too? Percy Spencer (1894–1970) was experimenting with a machine called a *magnetron* that produced microwaves, very small waves that transmit energy. Spencer discovered that a candy bar in his pocket had melted while he tested the microwaves. The idea for a fast-working oven was born.

Not all inventions happen by accident, of course. For example, the Wright Brothers worked for years to develop an airplane. Think about your favorite invention. Do you think any surprise discoveries brought it about?

Charles Goodyear, engraving by W. G. Jackman (Courtesy of The Library of Congress)

Tire collection (Courtesy of Lieven Volckaert, stock.xchng)

Vocabulary Words

cellulose nitrate......................pulpy material used in explosives and other substances

rubber.................................milky sap of the rubber tree, or the processed substance made from it

shatterproof glass..................form of safety glass designed to hold together if it breaks

vulcanization ....a process by which rubber is made stronger and more useful

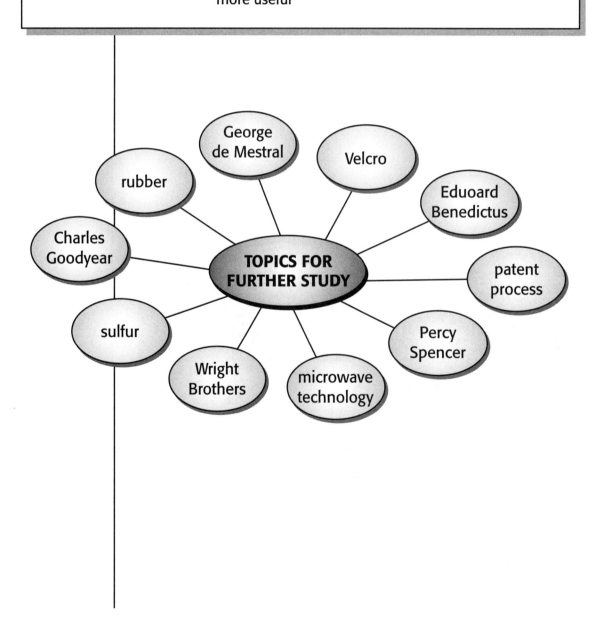

Bibliography

Gribben, John. *Almost Everyone's Guide to Science.* New Haven: Yale University Press, 1999.

Gribben, John. *The Scientists.* New York: Random House, 2002.

Hazen, Robert M., and James Trefil. *Science Matters.* New York: Doubleday, 1991.

Hellemans, Alexander, and Bryan Bunch. *The Timetables of Science.* New York: Simon and Schuster, 1988.

Hewitt, Paul G. *Conceptual Physics,* 6th ed. New York: HarperCollins, 1989.

Meadows, Jack. *The Great Scientists.* New York: Oxford University Press, 1996.

Panek, Richard. *Seeing and Believing.* New York: Penguin Books, 1998.

Simmons, John. *The Scientific 100.* Secaucus, NJ: Citadel Press, 1996.

Glossary

acceleration............................the change in an object's velocity over time

acid...sour-tasting liquid containing hydrogen ions (H+)

aerodynamics.........................study of the interaction of atmospheric gases with moving objects

alchemist...............................name for medieval chemists, some of whom claimed or sought the ability to turn other metals into gold

amber.....................................fossil form of resin (sticky liquid exuded by plants)

amperes.................................unit of electric current

amplifier.................................device that increases a signal

arc..segment of a curve

atom.......................................the smallest unit of an element

atomic mass...........................number of protons and neutrons in an atom's nucleus. Each individual atom's mass is a whole number, but because of isotopes, the average atomic mass for any element may be expressed as a decimal.

atomic structure.....................how atoms and molecules are built; the form of atoms

base.......................................substance that neutralizes acids, removing the hydrogen ions to form water

battery...................................device that produces an electric current through chemical reactions

calculus.................................branch of mathematics dealing with rates of change and related concepts

calx..crumbly residue produced by a chemical change when a mineral or metal has been heated

caustic...................................likely to burn or corrode substances it contacts

cellulose nitrate....................pulpy material used in explosives and other substances

chandelier..............................light fixture hanging from the ceiling

circuit breaker.......................switch that automatically interrupts the flow of electricity when a circuit becomes overloaded

compact disc (CD) ....device used for storing data in a digital format. A laser beam reads the sequence of pits in the disc.

compass ....instrument used to determine direction

compound ....in chemistry, a substance made up of the atoms of two or more elements bonded into molecules

conductors............................material through which heat and electricity flow easily

counterfeit ....imitation or copy of an original object designed to be accepted as genuine

crystal ....arrangement of matter in which the molecules are aligned in a regular, repeating structure

crystalline ....relating to crystal structure

daguerrotypes.......................photographs made on copper plates

defunct..................................no longer used

density ....a measure of how much matter is in a given space, or how "tightly packed" that matter is; represented by the formula density = mass/volume

diffusion ....gradual mixing of molecules due to random motion

digital video disc (DVD) ....device that records and stores data that can be shown visually

dynamo ....device in which an electromagnet produces a current

efficient.................................description of a high ratio of effort to production

effort.....................................application of force

electric circuit.......................closed path or loop of an electrical charge

electrical charge...................buildup or capacity of electricity to use force

electric current ....flow of an electrical charge

electricity..............................the force caused by the attraction between unlike charges and the repulsion between like forces

electrodes.............................a conductor through which electricity passes to enter part of a circuit, or where a charge is stored and emitted

electrolysis............................chemical change produced by passing electricity through an electrolyte

electrolyte.............................substances that produce ions in water and can carry electrical current electromagnetism ....type of radiation that travels in the form of waves

electron scanning
microscope............................device in which a beam of electrons contacts a specimen and creates a highly magnified image of it

electrons................................negatively charged particles in the shell around the nucleus of an atom

element..................................substance composed of one type of atom

experiment............................a controlled test of a hypothesis

filament.................................thin wire heated by electricity so that it glows and produces light

fluid.......................................substance that flows, usually but not always a gas or liquid

friction...................................the force resisting motion

fulcrum ....pivot point of a lever

fuse..device designed to protect a circuit by melting when overloaded

galaxy ....group of stars orbiting a common center. Galaxies also contain gas, dust, and solid objects.

gas...state of matter in which molecules have no definite shape and fill whatever space is available

geometry...............................branch of mathematics dealing with shapes, points, lines, angles, and so on.

gravity...................................force of attraction between objects based on their mass

heart rate ....frequency of "beats" or contractions of the heart

heat.......................................form of energy resulting from particle motion

high-tech...............................nickname for specially designed, advanced devices

horsepower...........................unit of power equivalent to 746 watts

hydroxide.............................chemical compound containing a hydroxyl group, OH (oxygen and hydrogen)

Industrial Revolution..........historical period during which the means of production shifted from home manufacture to machines in factories. The Industrial Revolution is generally considered to have begun in England in the late eighteenth century and lasted well into the 1800s.

inertia	resistance to a change in state of motion
inflammable	catches fire easily
instantaneous	occurring at a point in time
insulators	materials that inhibit the flow of heat or electrical current
ion	an atom with an electrical charge
isotopes	atoms of the same element containing different numbers of neutrons
keystone	central wedge-shaped stone in an arch or the central idea in a theory or argument
laser	acronym for "**l**ight **a**mplification by **s**timulated **e**mission of **r**adiation," a device that produces a concentrated beam of light
Leiden jar	device for building up and storing static electricity
lever	simple machine consisting of a bar and a fixed point (fulcrum) upon which it may pivot
light	visible part of the electromagnetic spectrum
light-gathering microscope	optical device used for magnifying small objects by refracting light through the use of lenses
lightning	natural high-energy electric discharge in the atmosphere
liquid	state of matter having definite volume but taking the shape of the container in which it is confined
load	mass or object to be moved or lifted
lodestone	magnetized piece of magnetite rock
loudspeaker	device that converts electrical signals into sound
machine	a device designed to aid the application of applied force or to help do work
magnet	an object that attracts substances containing certain metals, especially iron
magnetic field	the space around a magnet where its force is in effect
magnetism	having the properties of a magnet
magnification	to increase the size or image of an object

mass..a measure of the quantity of matter

matter...anything that occupies space

mechanical advantage.......ratio of the output to the input forces. *Mechanical advantage* describes the effect or efficiency of a machine.

mechanics.............................study of the effect of forces upon objects

medieval.................................referring to the Middle Ages, a historical period in European history often considered approximately A.D. 500–1500

metal.......................................the set of elements to the left of a line on the periodic table. Most metals are shiny, conduct heat and electricity, and have relatively high melting points.

Milky Way..............................spiral galaxy containing our solar system

millennium...........................a period of a thousand years

mineral...................................naturally occurring inorganic (not from living things) solid substance with a specific chemical composition and crystal structure

molecule................................two or more atoms bonded together

negative plate.....................in photography, a piece of film on which an image formed after a chemical reaction. Dark areas of the object depicted appear light and light areas appear dark. When a photograph is printed, the areas of the image become a positive, or actual likeness.

neutrons................................subatomic particle in the nucleus carrying no electrical charge

Newtonian telescope.........telescope that magnifies an image by reflecting light off mirrors

Nobel Prize............................international prize awarded for outstanding achievement in a variety of fields

non-Newtonian fluid..........fluid whose viscosity (resistance to flow) depends on force applied

nucleus...................................in a cell, the part separated by a membrane and containing most of the cell's DNA. In an atom, a positively charged mass containing protons and neutrons.

oxygen....................................gas that makes up about 21% of Earth's atmosphere paradox.................................a contradiction, often occurring when two statements appear to be true alone but seem to disagree when considered together

particles................................tiny pieces; minute parts

patent...................................the legal statement giving an inventor exclusive rights to make and sell an invention

Periodic Table
of the Elements....................a chart organizing the elements by atomic structure and chemical properties

pH scale................................scale that indicates whether a solution is acidic or alkaline (base)

phenakistoscope ....device in which a spinning disk is observed through another disk with slits cut out. The observer has the illusion of seeing a motion picture.

phenomenon.........................an occurrence or fact

phlogiston.............................non-existent substance that early chemists mistakenly believed to be released in the form of flame when things burned

phonograph ....machine used to play back sound recorded on records, hard plastic discs with grooves. As a record turns, a needle travels through the grooves, vibrating and reproducing the recorded sound.

physical science ....any of the branches of science dealing with matter and energy, often grouped into chemistry, physics, and Earth and space sciences

physics..................................branch of science concerned with the interaction between matter and energy

pollen....................................material produced by anthers of flowers that is the male element in fertilization

positive image......................in photography, the image or actual likeness. Compare to *negative,* which carries the opposite image so that dark areas represent light sections and vice versa.

prism ....triangular clear material (like glass) that separates white light into its colors

protons ....subatomic particle in the nucleus carrying a positive electrical charge pulley.....................................simple machine consisting of a wheel with a groove through which a rope or chain passes. Pulleys are used for changing direction of force or lifting objects.

pulse.......................................the throbbing of blood vessels caused the beating of the heart

quantum ....a unit of a quantity that operates as a discrete bundle. Quantum theory states that energy radiates in "packages" of specific amounts.

radiation...............................energy emission by means of waves or particles

radioactive ....describes material that emits radiation from the nuclei (plural of nucleus) of its atoms

radioactivity.........................process in which an element breaks apart or decays to become another element, emitting high-frequency waves

renaissance ....a revival, a reawakening of cultural achievement

resin.......................................substance produced by plants (and in modern times by human engineers) used to make a variety of products

retina.....................................light-sensitive layer of cells in the eye

rocket engine.......................engine that propels a vehicle by the combustion of material and ejection of the gases produced

rubber ....milky sap of the rubber tree, or the processed substance made from it

rust...scaly result of iron combining with oxygen

shatterproof glass...............form of safety glass designed to hold together if it breaks

short circuit ....when two points in an electrical circuit accidentally meet so the current travels between them instead of on the intended pathway

shuttle spacecraft...............vehicles designed to enter space and return so they can be flown multiple times

simple machine ....simple device that changes the direction or amount of force applied to an object

smith ....a metalworker

solid.......................................state of matter having definite shape and volume solution .... evenly distributed mixture of two or more substances

space junk .... orbiting remnants of man-made objects in space

space station .... a long-term manned satellite designed for scientific research

spectrum .... sequence or range of energy by wavelength

speed .... rate at which distance is traveled by an object

speed of light .... approximately 300,000 kilometers per second (186,000 miles per second) in a vacuum

sphere .... solid round figure

static electricity .... accumulation of electrical charge

steam engine .... machine that uses the energy of steam to produce mechanical energy

subatomic particles .... the components of atoms, any form of matter smaller than the atom itself

superpowers .... very powerful nations that are dominant in world affairs

telegraph .... communication device that sends electrical signals through wires across distances

thaumatrope .... toy that simulates motion by quickly alternating pictures from one side of a card to the other

thermodynamics .... study of the relationship between heat and other forms of energy

three-wire electric supply .... system used to supply electricity safely to users so that more than one device may be operated at a time

transformer .... device that causes an increase or decrease in current

transmitter .... device that converts sound or other form of information into electrical signals and radiates it to receivers

vacuum .... a space empty of air

vacuum tube .... a sealed tube in an electronic device through which electrons flow

variable .... In scientific experiments, something a researcher changes to collect data about its effect.

velocity.............................the speed and direction of an object over time

video cassette
recorder (VCR) ....device that records and plays video programming using magnetic tape contained within a cartridge or cassette

visible light ....the part of the electromagnetic spectrum perceivable to human eyes

visualize.............................to create a mental picture of

voltage ....electrical pressure, or the potential difference of an electrical charge

vulcanization.......................a process by which rubber is made stronger and more useful

watts..................................unit of power

waves.................................energy that travels across space as motion or disturbance

wedge.................................simple machine of one or more inclined planes, used for applying force

wireless
communication...................general term for sending signals without wires connecting the transmitter and receiver

work...................................product of force and the distance it is applied. When an object changes its position as the result of force, work has been done.

X rays................................radiation of a specific high-frequency wavelength in which the photons have high penetrating power and can pass through solid objects

ziggurats............................towers built by the ancient Assyrians and Babylonians

zoetrope.............................a rotating wheel of drawings that simulates a motion picture

Notes

Notes